A Cruising Cook's Guide to Mexico

UP-TO-DATE INFORMATION ON PROVISIONING AND COOKING IN PACIFIC MEXICO

A Cruising Cook's Guide to Mexico

UP-TO-DATE INFORMATION ON PROVISIONING AND COOKING IN PACIFIC MEXICO

Heather Stockard

Seaworthy
PUBLICATIONS

Seaworthy Publications, Inc. • PORT WASHINGTON, WISCONSIN

A Cruising Cook's Guide to Mexico
Up-to-date Information on Provisioning and Cooking in Pacific Mexico
by Heather Stockard

Copyright ©2008 by Heather Stockard

ISBN 978-1-892399-25-0

Published in the USA by: Seaworthy Publications, Inc.
626 W. Pierre
Port Washington, WI 53074
PHONE: 262-268-9250
FAX: 262-268-9208
E-MAIL: orders@seaworthy.com
WEB: www.seaworthy.com

PHOTO CREDITS: Chris and Heather Stockard except as noted

COVER DESIGN: Ken Quant, Broad Reach Marketing & Design, Mequon, Wisconsin

Library of Congress Cataloging-in-Publication Data

Stockard, Heather, 1954-
    A cruising cook's guide to Mexico : up-to-date information on provisioning and cooking in Pacific Mexico / Heather Stockard.
        p. cm.
    Includes index.
    ISBN 978-1-892399-25-0 (pbk. : alk. paper) 1. Cookery, Marine. 2. Cookery--Mexico. 3. Boats and boating. I. Title.

TX840.M7S76 2008
641.5972--dc22
                            2007026531

DEDICATION

To our families, for their "legacy" of sailing, and for all they have done to make it possible for us to pursue our dreams.

ACKNOWLEDGEMENTS

Many people helped make this book possible. Thanks go to the many friends and cruisers who were willing to share information and expertise with me, including Leslie on SunBreak, Geri on Lady Geraldine, Leslie and Philip on Carina, John on Pelagic, Kathy on Ahwahnee, Mike on Tortue, Rita on Overheated, Jennifer on Nuestra Isla, Marilyn on Tortuga, Mary on Allegro, Sandy on Pegasus, Renie on Scarlett O'Hara, Judy on Deja Two, Karin and Marike on Quoddy's Run, Linda on Williwaw, and Mary on Angelos.

Special thanks go to Joan Stockard for her support, help with logistics, and thoughtful editing.

And most of all, my heartfelt thanks to my husband Chris for being a sounding board, for his support, editing, photography, and computer skills, and especially for washing mountains of dishes during the recipe testing phase aboard Legacy.

Contents

Introduction

WHEREVER CRUISERS GATHER, they talk not only about sailing but also about food. During our first three years cruising in Pacific Mexico aboard our Saga 43, Legacy, I had many conversations with other cruisers about food, cooking, provisioning, and about the things in Mexico that had taken them by surprise. I cannot count the number of times I heard: "I wish I'd known...", "Why did I think that...", and "Everyone told me that...." Misconceptions and surprises related to food, cooking, and provisioning are common among cruisers.

By the time my husband, Chris, and I had been cruising for a few months, we came to a startling realization: People eat everywhere! Yes, it's true; just about everywhere you go, you will find that people eat and you can buy food. You may not know the name of the food in the local language or how to prepare it, but you won't starve to death. That realization and the experience I gained in my first three years in Mexico prompted me to write this book. My goal in writing this book is to help you learn to shop for food in Mexico and prepare delicious meals using locally available ingredients, and to learn how to adapt your own recipes to use Mexican ingredients.

DON'T BELIEVE EVERYTHING YOU ARE TOLD:

Many cruisers headed to Mexico have read older provisioning guides or guides to worldwide cruising, or attended seminars that gave lists of what items to take to Mexico. Remember to take any source of information, including this book, with a grain of salt. Use the information along with your own knowledge and judgment to figure out the best course of action for you.

Many older guides recommend taking six months worth of food and paper products to Mexico. Times have changed; it's not necessary to load down your boat. In the 21st century, Costco and Wal-Mart have come to Mexico. In larger cities you will find most of the items that you need in large Mexican grocery or discount stores. In smaller communities you may be limited to what the locals use, but you will always find something to eat. See the chapters on Ingredients and Cooking Terms, and Things to Bring from the U.S. for more details about availability of ingredients and what items you might want to bring with you. Remember that everything you bring with you takes up room and adds weight to your boat. Even if you had unlimited room, excess items are likely to spoil or go stale, resulting in wasted money, space, and time.

Also, remember that while you may adjust how you cook slightly, you are unlikely to change drastically how you eat just because you are cruising in Mexico. Plan to cook your favorite recipes and eat your favorite foods, but try some new local foods as well. You may even find some new favorite foods by experimenting. In the U.S. the grocery store flour tortillas we bought had all the taste and appeal of eating newspaper. Good for holding a tasty filling, but of no interest themselves. A fresh, warm flour tortilla straight off the grill at the *tortillería* is a sensual treat.

We often hear funny stories about what foods cruisers have brought with them based on recommendations of some guide or seminar. Top Ramen is frequently recommended as a cruising food. One cruiser, Mary, took that recommendation seriously and bought a Costco case of Top Ramen before leaving for Mexico. She had it stored everywhere in her boat, including the engine room. To make matters worse, she and her husband weren't even fond of Top Ramen. Mary ended up emailing all her friends soliciting recipes to help her use up all of those packages of ramen noodles. And, by the way, if you really want ramen noodles, you can buy them in just about any Mexican grocery store.

> ### Key Recommendations:
>
> - Don't load down your boat with six months' of food
> - Don't buy large amounts of unfamiliar foods to bring
> - Don't expect to suddenly revamp the way you eat
> - Do select a few key items to bring with you
> - Do be adventurous and try some local or unfamiliar foods

CRUISING PACIFIC MEXICO IS DIFFERENT:

Many cruising galley and provisioning books focus on long ocean passages or worldwide locations. As many cruisers have discovered, Pacific Mexico is accessible to almost any boater, and the type of cruising is a bit different from cruising, say, the South Pacific. These differences affect how you will cook and provision as well.

First, in Mexico you will have frequent opportunities to re-provision. I start out the cruising season with a good stock of basic supplies, and plan on a major re-provisioning expedition about once a month. At any time, we have 4–6 weeks worth of meat in the freezer and canned goods and other staples on hand. Every one to two weeks, depending on our cruising area, we replenish produce, dairy products, tortillas, and other perishables.

Another difference in Mexican cruising is the length of passages. While many cruising cookbooks extensively discuss offshore cooking, passages in Mexico are typically 12 to 48 hours, with occasional 72-hour passages possible. For short passages, I prefer to cook in advance and warm up meals on the stove or in the microwave. That strategy works well in Mexico, even if it wouldn't be practical on passage to the Marquesas.

For most cruisers in Mexico, cruising is a seasonal activity. You'll find that only a small percentage of cruisers summer over in Pacific Mexico. Those that do are mainly in marinas, or cruising in the far northern Sea of Cortez. Other cruisers sail home, or leave their boats in marinas or on the hard while they travel home, visit family, go back to work, travel in the cool highlands of interior Mexico, or otherwise while away the hottest months. While in Mexico, Chris and I generally cruise about eight months of the year, leaving Legacy on the hard in San Carlos from June through September. This seasonal pattern offers the opportunity to return to the U.S. and indulge in any foods that you haven't been able to find in Mexico.

ABOUT THIS BOOK:

This book doesn't pretend to be a complete guide to outfitting and preparing a cruising galley; there are many books available that address that issue well. If you'd like more detail about Legacy's galley equipment, see Appendix: What Would You Find in Legacy's Galley? This book aims to help those who are cruising, or traveling by RV or other land means in Pacific Mexico to use local ingredients to eat well. In it, you will find local information about major cruising destinations in Pacific Mexico. Not every tienda is mentioned; I focus on a few in each location that are popular with cruisers and are stable enough that they are likely to be around from year to year.

In providing recipes, I assume that you are already familiar with cooking basics. I have personally tested all of these recipes aboard Legacy. Most of them use ingredients that are readily available in Mexico, at least in large grocery stores, although a few use ingredients that are on my list of items to bring from the U.S. You will find that some recipes can be easily prepared in the smallest of galleys, but some require more space and equipment. Even on Legacy, I prepare some recipes only on special occasions. When selecting recipes to include in this book, I tried to create a useful mix of dishes and to eliminate any recipes that were overly fussy. Except for baked goods, these recipes are relatively tolerant of approximate measures and

> ### Not everyone cooks
>
> Although most cruisers in Mexico eat well, not everyone is willing to cook. We met one cruising couple who ate out frequently and for whom cooking involved opening a can and heating the contents on the stove. We met them several months into their cruise and the lady of the boat still hadn't figured out how to light their propane oven. It's obviously possible to cruise that way, but nothing enhances my pleasure at being in a beautiful anchorage more than enjoying an easy and delicious meal.

cooks that don't follow directions precisely. I encourage you to use these recipes as a starting point, and modify them to suit your needs and tastes.

ADDITIONS, CORRECTIONS, AND CHANGES:

Although all the information is as current as I can make it in the fall of 2006, things in Mexico change frequently. If you find information that is no longer correct, have a special *tienda* to recommend, or have questions about this book, please email me at stockard@123mail.net. I will use your additions, corrections, suggestions, and changes to prepare future editions of this book.

General Provisioning Tips

SHOPPING IN MEXICO CAN BE FUN, entertaining, challenging, and sometimes downright frustrating. The challenges result from cultural differences, different shopping styles, and the unfamiliar brands, foods, and preparations found in Mexican stores. But since many of us travel to experience different cultures we should welcome these challenges. I find that food is a universal language. Provisioning offers many opportunities to interact with locals and provides a window into the Mexican culture. To ease your passage into Mexican culture, this chapter includes background information, what to expect at stores, shopping strategies, and useful items to have on board.

CASH AND CURRENCY

Let's begin with a discussion of cash and currency. While some larger stores may accept credit cards, many cruisers choose to use cash for all purchases except those at major marinas or resorts to minimize the risk of credit card fraud. So starting with a quick review of Mexican currency, remember that the basic unit is the peso, with subdivisions called centavos. There are 100 centavos to the peso and you will see 10-, 20-, and 50-centavo coins. You can pretty much ignore centavos as a 50-centavo coin is only worth about a nickel. About the only place you'll even get them in your change is at large grocery stores. At large stores, clerks will sometimes ask if you want to donate your centavos to education.

In the mid-2000's, the exchange rate was between 10 and 11 pesos per U.S. dollar. In casual settings, cruisers generally use a 10 peso to the dollar exchange rate for simplicity or as a quick estimate of price. You will commonly see 1-, 2-, 5-, 10-, and sometimes 20-peso coins. You will see bills in 20-, 50-, 100-, 200-, and 500-peso denominations. Frequently ATMs will dispense 500-peso notes, which can be hard to change in smaller towns or stores. Cruisers sometimes refer to them as "dread 500s".

Use 500-peso notes at large grocery stores, gas stations, fuel docks, or busy restaurants and hoard your smaller bills for daily use.

Most cruisers use ATMs, called *cajero automático* or *caja permanente*, to get pesos. You will occasionally hear stories of ATMs that run out of cash but still debit your account. By contacting your bank at home, you can get this charge reversed but it may take several weeks. To avoid the problem, try to use ATMs at a bank and only during banking hours. Then, if the ATM eats your card or fails to give you cash, you can go into the bank for assistance. Especially avoid ATMs late in the weekend or early Monday morning when their cash supply may be depleted. If you must use an ATM during off-hours, try a small cash withdrawal first to make sure the machine has money before making a significant withdrawal. The ATMs at major banks you'll see in cruising ports generally have instructions in English as well as Spanish. Most will charge a fee of 4–8 pesos (U.S. $0.40–0.80) for a cash withdrawal. Some North American banks charge excessive fees for withdrawals from foreign ATMs; others charge nothing if you keep a substantial balance in your accounts. Check with your home bank for charges and consider changing banks if they are unreasonable. The Spanish phrase for cash withdrawal is *retiro de efectivo*. One difference from U.S. ATMs is that when your card is returned you should immediately remove it from the slot. After a brief period, as little as ten seconds, your card may be sucked back into the machine and retained. If this happens you must contact the bank to get your card back. This is another reason to use ATMs located at banks.

Another option is to change your U.S. or Canadian currency or travelers checks at a bank or money exchange business (*casa de cambio*) or get credit card advances at a bank. Bank lines tend to be long, so look around when you enter to see if there is a "take a number" machine. The banks you will encounter most frequently are Banamex, Bancomer, Santander Serfin, ScotiaBank, HSBC, and Banorte. Also, many businesses in coastal areas (particularly the Baja and northern mainland coast) will take U.S. dollars for your purchase and give you change in pesos. This can be convenient, but sometimes the exchange rate is very bad. Look around to see if they have a posted exchange rate.

One special note for those bringing boats down the outside of the Baja: Vendors in the small communities along the Pacific coast of the Baja prefer U.S. dollars for fuel, for meals, even for tips. Bring a large supply of small U.S. bills —ones, fives, and a few twenties for fuel and other large purchases.

One additional note on cash: We don't routinely carry our credit cards with us, preferring to leave them secured on board. We carry our currency and ATM cards in a small waterproof case on a cord around our necks rather than in a purse or wallet. Some areas of Mexico have pickpockets or bag-slashers. I did get a bag slashed in the central mercado of Mazatlan during a busy Carnival weekend. Luckily it was only my shopping bag, so the would-be thief found only my shopping list and a few onions rather than the wallet he or she was expecting!

WHAT IF I DON'T SPEAK SPANISH?

You'll find the Mexican people very helpful and they will appreciate even your stumbling efforts to speak their language. With just a few words under your belt, you'll be able

ATM kiosks are common in medium- and large-size communities. By local custom, patrons wait outside the kiosk door until an ATM is available.

to make purchases. "Please (*por favor*)" and "thank you (*gracias*)" will get you a long way. "How much is it? (*¿Cuánto cuesta?*)" is another useful phrase. Don't worry about the numbers initially. Many clerks, especially in tourist businesses, know numbers in English. Otherwise, they may show you the number on the cash register or punch it into a calculator. Barring those options, you can also ask "Please write it (*escribalo, por favor*)". Other useful phrases are "I don't understand (*no entiendo*)" or "I don't speak Spanish (*no hablo español*)" delivered with an apologetic smile. A useful technique is to write out your shopping list in advance and translate it into Spanish using the Ingredients and Cooking Terms chapter of this book or a Spanish-English dictionary. Not only will that help you reading labels in the grocery store, but you can show your written list to a store worker if you need assistance.

A QUICK REVIEW OF THE METRIC SYSTEM:

Mexico uses the metric system primarily, although you will see some products sold in quart, half-gallon, or pound packages. In case you've forgotten your junior high science classes, here's a quick review of the metric system:

- A liter is just a little more than a quart. There are 3.875 liters in a gallon.
- A kilo is 2.2 pounds. So a pound is a little less than half a kilo (media kilo). There are 1000 grams in a kilo. Meats and deli items are frequently sold in 100 gram units, which are a little less than 1/4 pound.
- There are 28 grams in an ounce.
- A meter is a little more than a yard (3.28 feet).
- A kilometer is a little more than a half mile (.62 miles)

Look in Substitutions, Conversions, and Rules of Thumb for charts to help you convert pesos/kilo to dollars/pound and pesos/liter to dollars/gallon.

TYPES OF MARKETS:

You will encounter a wide variety of grocery stores in Mexico. The generic name for a small shop is *tienda*, though that often refers to a convenience store. In the smallest *tiendas*, you will probably see less food than you'd find in the average U.S. kitchen. Another term you'll see is *tienda de abarrotes* or grocery store.

At the other extreme, in large communities you may find Mexican versions of U.S. big box stores such as Wal-Mart, Costco, and Sam's Club. In larger towns, you'll see major Mexican grocery chains such as Commercial, Soriana, Ley's, Gigante or CCC. However, something called a supermarket (*supermercado*) may be only a convenience store or small grocery store. In some communities, especially small towns, you may also encounter a government-run grocery store known as an ISSSTE store. ISSSTE is the acronym for the government social agency that operates the store. Anyone can shop at an ISSSTE store, which generally sell a full range of basic food items.

Specialty shops are also common in Mexico. When provisioning, you can check out the local bakery (*panadería*), butcher shop (*carnecería*), produce shop (*fruitería*), fish store (*pescadería*), and the tortilla maker (*tortillería*). Often these specialty stores have better versions of the same foods that you find in the large grocery chains. Fish may be fresher and meat more tender. Check with other cruisers for their favorites.

Most communities also have a central *mercado*. In smaller towns, the *mercado* will only be open on market day. In other towns the *mercado* is busy six or seven days a week, with produce stands, *panaderías, carnecerías*, and a variety of stalls selling clothes, plastic ware, prepared foods, hardware, and other items. The first time I went in search of a *mercado*, I couldn't find it because I was expecting open-air stalls. The mercado is likely a nondescript concrete building with small businesses opening onto the street around the perimeter. It's only when you peer into one of the entrances to the building interior that you'll see the maze of stalls inside. Vendor stalls are usually organized by what they are offering for sale, so the vegetable stalls are together, as are the clothing, hardware, and other classifications.

Veggie trucks that visit marinas, RV parks, or street corners in small towns are another convenient source of food in Mexico. Many veggie trucks will have the nicest fruits and vegetables around, but will be more expensive than large supermarkets. Some also carry eggs, tortillas, *bolillos* (bread rolls), and other items. A few enterprising veggie truck owners also offer homemade tacos, chile rellenos, fresh-squeezed orange juice, and salsa to their customers. Seafood vendors often sell off trucks as well or by carrying coolers through marinas. In some anchorages, you may be approached by fishermen in *pangas*. This is a great way to purchase, or sometimes trade for, fresh fish or lobster. Some marinas are visited regularly by other vendors such as the "water truck" and the "beer truck."

WHAT TO EXPECT AT THE STORE:

At many larger stores, you may not carry bags or parcels other than a purse. Just inside or outside the entrance of the store, look for a sign that says "*Paqueteria*". Give your bags or purchases to the clerk behind the counter. She will put them in a cubbyhole and usually give you a numbered tag that matches the cubbyhole. When you're done shopping, exchange the tag for your parcels. Sometimes there will be a tip jar on the counter where you can leave a couple of pesos. If there is no counter labeled "*Paqueteria*", there may be a security guard by the entrance who will motion you to leave your bags in his custody.

You may want to bring your own canvas shopping or tote bags to the store with you. Your groceries will be bagged in flimsy plastic bags which are difficult and uncomfortable to carry any distance. If you are taking the bus or even just carrying your groceries from a taxi to the boat, it's generally nice to have a tote or knapsack that can hold several plastic bags. Also, I'll sometimes carry a folding insulated bag to bring milk and meat back to the boat from the store. Insulated bags are sold in many of the larger chain stores. You will frequently see them displayed near the ice cream case. Once you are finished with your shopping, you can either retrieve your bags from the Paqueteria before going through the checkout line or pick them up as you exit the store and transfer your groceries from the cart to your bags. Especially in smaller

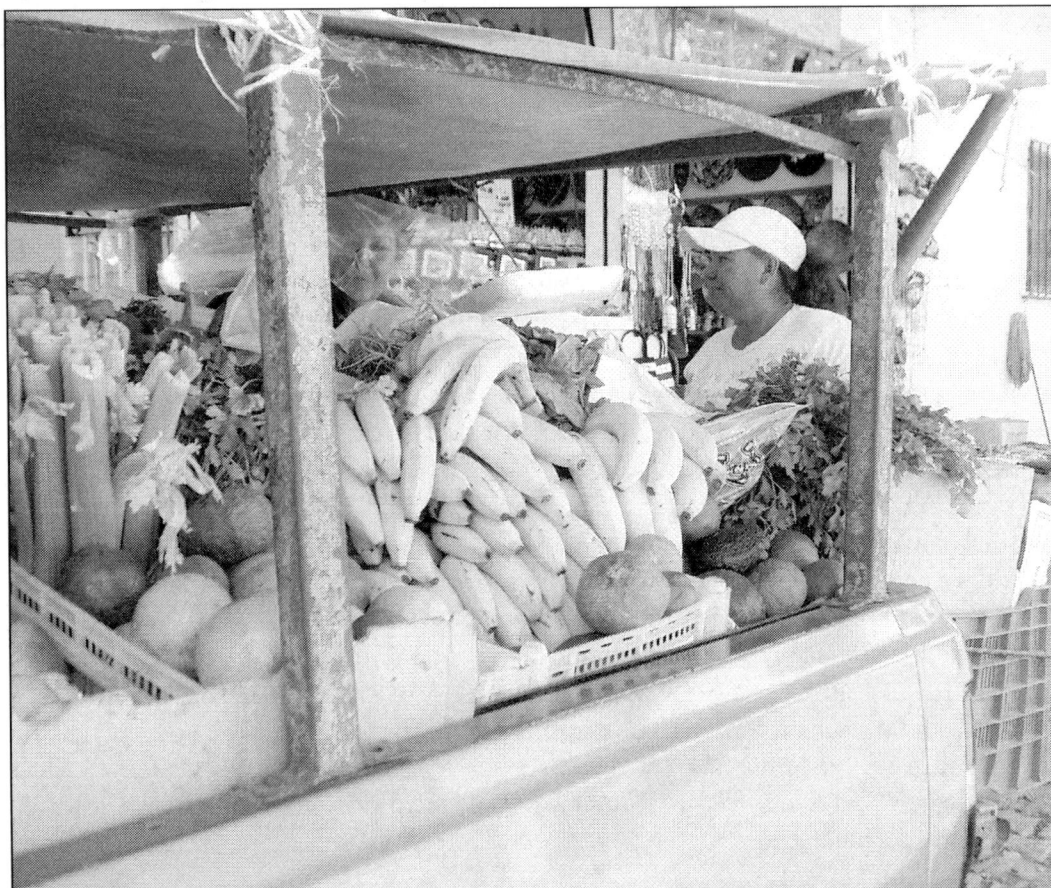

Produce trucks are often a convenient way to purchase fruits and vegetables. Quality of the produce is frequently better than that found in small *tiendas,* and the vendor may be able to get you special items by arrangement.

towns, you should also take an egg container to the store. In larger stores you will find eggs packed in cartons as at home. However eggs are also sold individually by the kilo and smaller stores may offer only bulk eggs. Believe me, it's no fun trying to get eggs back to the boat intact if you are carrying them piled in a plastic bag!

Bagboys at the store often are not paid a salary and survive on tips alone. I usually tip them from a peso or two for bagging a few items to ten pesos or more for bagging a large order and taking it to a taxi for me. If you are driving a car, at malls or other large stores you may see security guards in the parking lot. They will direct you into a vacant space, keep an eye on the cars in the lots, and hold traffic so you can back out of the space when you leave. They appreciate a small tip for their services.

AT THE PANADERÍA:

When you enter the bakery, or the bakery section of a large chain store, look around for a stack of trays and tongs. Take one of each and start helping yourself to delicious goodies. Don't hold back, because Mexican baked goods are very inexpensive. However, plan to use up the baked goods within a couple of days because they go stale quickly.

In the baskets, bins, or trays of the *panadería* you will see cookies (*galleta*), sweet rolls (*pan dulce*), bread rolls (*bolillos*), and bread (*pan*). When you're done, take your tray to the counter where a clerk will bag them. At a large chain store, you'll pay for them with the rest of your purchases. In a specialty shop, you'll take the bagged items to the cashier (*caja*).

SAFE FOOD AND WATER:

While sanitation conditions in the coastal towns that cruisers visit are relatively good, we still take some basic precautions to avoid illness. First, take a good look at the store, restaurant, or cart where you are buying food to ensure that things seem to be reasonably

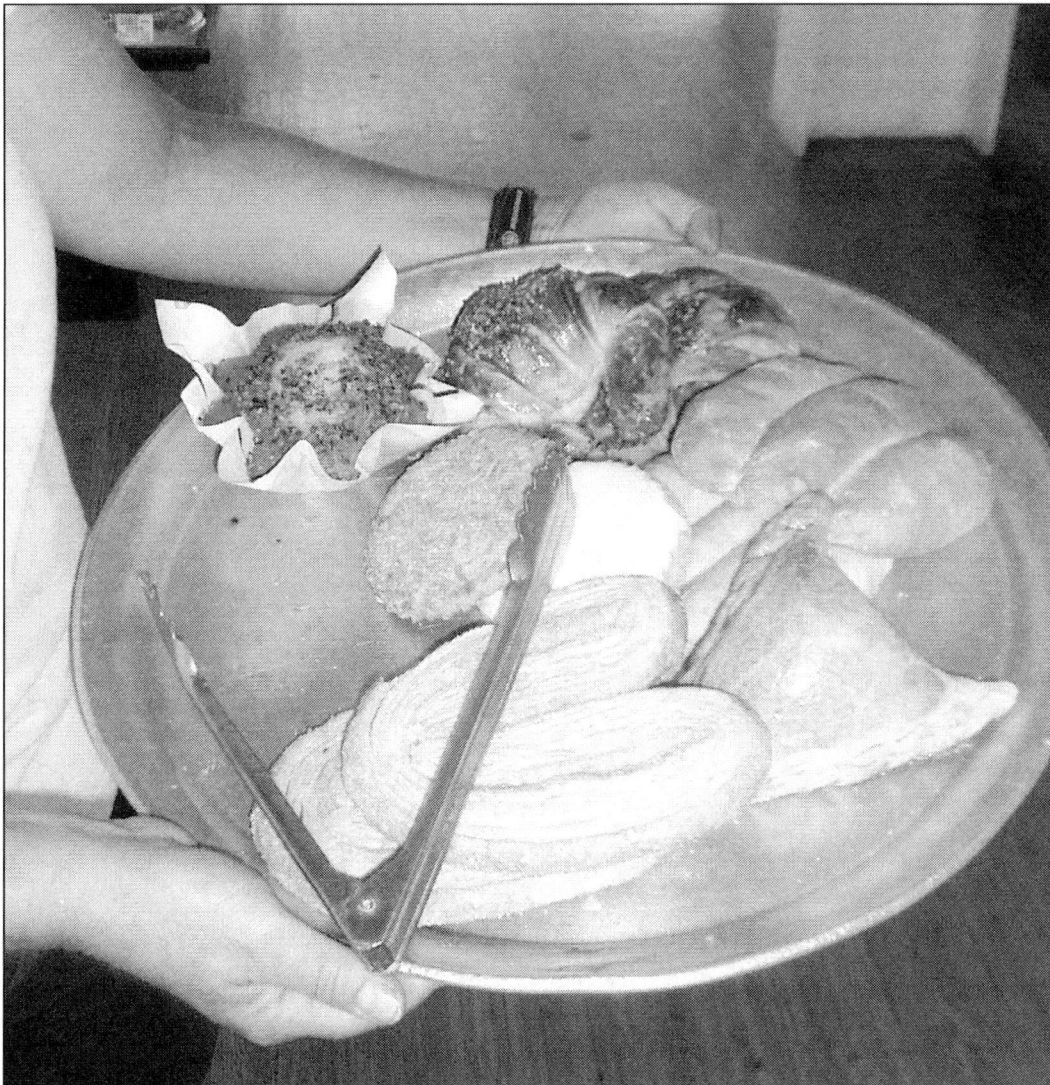

At the *panadería*, take a tray and tongs to select baked goods from the displays. Mexican baked goods tend to be less sweet than those found in the U.S. and Canada, and are very inexpensive. Most items cost 2–3 pesos.

clean. Make sure to cook all unpasteurized dairy products. Any other suspect foods should be also thoroughly cooked. If a prepared meal is questionable, squeezing lime juice over the food is believed to reduce the risk of illness. However, knock on wood, we've rarely been sick from eating or drinking in Mexico. Most restaurants, and even taco stands, use bottled water (*agua purificado*) in all food and beverage preparation. Just about all ice (*hielo*—pronounced like "yellow") comes from the ice plant, which uses purified water. Below are some commonsense precautions for cruisers:

Disinfecting produce:

As soon as I get back to the boat, I soak all produce in a bleach-water solution. Add a couple of tablespoons of chlorine bleach (5% sodium hypochlorite without extra additives) to a gallon of water. Soak all produce for 5 minutes, and then set it on clean dish towels to air dry before storing. Cantaloupe and other foods that can trap dirt require extra cleaning. In addition to the bleach-water soak, you should scrub cantaloupe skin with soap and water to remove any dirt that could contain salmonella. As an alternative to using bleach, there are iodine-based commercial disinfecting products available in the produce section of most large grocery stores.

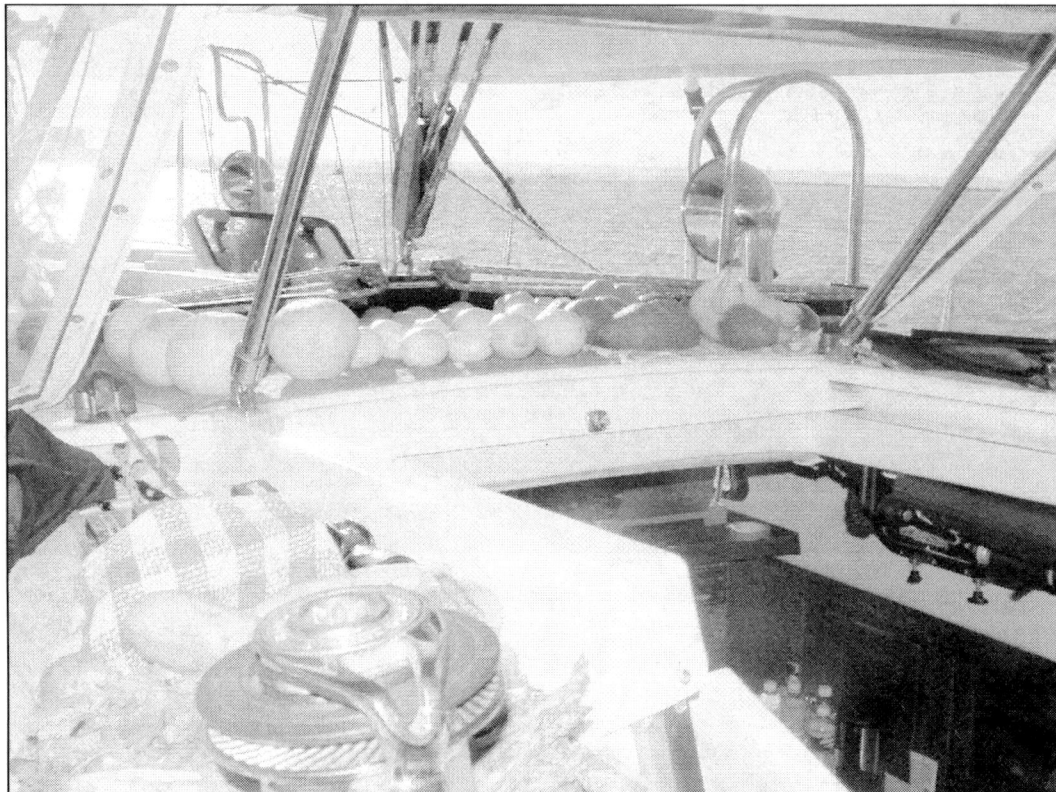

Aboard Legacy, we allow produce to air-dry after being disinfected in a bleach-water solution. In addition to cleaning the produce, the bleach soak also seems to extend the storage life of some fruits and vegetables.

After removing my produce from the bleach water, I frequently throw my kitchen sponges into the basin of solution to soak for a few minutes and kill bacteria. Another sanitizing method is to wet your sponges and put them in the microwave for five minutes. In any case, have enough sponges on board that you can replace them frequently.

Ensuring safe water:

The majority of cruisers use watermakers when underway or at anchor to ensure a safe supply of drinking water. Most manufacturers recommend that watermakers not be used in marinas to avoid contamination by petroleum products. While larger marinas usually have water that is safe to drink, ask other cruisers if they use the water before filling your tanks. We always chlorinate water that we add to our tanks from marina docks to ensure safety, and usually filter it as well. Chlorine also inhibits bacteria and algae growth in your water tanks. A simple particle filter can be purchased in most Mexican communities or at Home Depot in the States. Some cruisers also use a ceramic 5-micron filter to remove contaminants or an activated charcoal filter to remove off flavors.

Before chlorinating tanks, ensure that your tanks are not made of aluminum (since chlorine can cause oxidation in aluminum tanks) and that your watermaker fresh water flush setup doesn't preclude the use of chlorine. To chlorinate your tanks effectively, it's important to know how much water you are treating. The first step is to know how many tanks you have and the capacity of each. It's also helpful if you have a way to gauge how much water is left in the tank. For our main tank, we added a removable plug to the top and have a wooden dowel with 5-gallon markings that we calibrated by adding measured amounts of water to the tank. When filling your tanks, add one teaspoon of bleach for each ten gallons of water being treated. In Substitutions, Conversions, and Rules of Thumb, you will find a chart to easily calculate the amount of bleach you need to add to your tanks.

Another option is to purchase purified water for use in your boat water tanks or just for drinking water. In almost all communities, purified water is available in one-gallon or five-gallon containers. In some marinas or anchorages, you can have bottled water delivered directly to your boat. Ice made with purified water is available at most marinas and many stores.

Sanitizing water tanks: In addition to chlorinating water, we take the extra step of cleaning and sanitizing our water tanks periodically. I sanitize the tanks about every six months or at the beginning of each cruising season. This step keeps our water sweet tasting, rather than getting the common stale, musty flavor of tank water. To sanitize a tank, first empty it of all water. Then mix 1/8 cup bleach and one teaspoon of dish detergent in a couple of cups of water. Add the bleach-detergent mixture to the tank along with about ten gallons of warm water. Rock the boat to make sure that the solution is well-mixed in the tank. Next, open each faucet on the boat (including showers) until the sanitizing solution appears. A chlorine smell is a good indicator. Don't forget the cockpit shower and other less obvious faucets. Let the solution stand in the lines for at least one hour to ensure disinfection. Then run all of the sanitizing

Agua purificada is delivered daily to boats in Marina Mazatlan. Some boats will use dock water in one tank for showering and washing, and fill another tank with bottled water for drinking and cooking.

solution out of the tank and follow with at least two complete flushes of the tank. Repeat with each water tank on board. Obviously, this task should be undertaken when in a marina with plentiful, safe supplies of water!

USEFUL ITEMS TO HAVE ABOARD

While I won't go into a full discussion of equipping the galley on a cruising boat, I want to highlight a few items that I've found especially useful for cruising in Mexican waters.

FoodSaver:

I wouldn't go cruising without my vacuum packer! I use it for meats going into the freezer, for fish we catch along the way, and for packing spare parts for storage. We also used the FoodSaver to protect items that we had the liferaft manufacturer pack into our raft, such as prescription drugs and important papers.

Other small electric appliances:

You may want to have a couple of other small appliances to use in marinas, or at anchor or underway if you have an inverter or generator to make 110-volt power. In addition to the built-in microwave, the ones that I choose to carry are a small food processor, a hand mixer, and a small rice cooker. A small food processor is useful for making soups and salsas. The rice cooker allows us to enjoy rice as often as we like without heating up the cabin. Other cruisers choose to carry coffee makers, toasters, blenders, or bread machines. Your choices will be dictated by the amount of storage room you have available and what is most important to you.

Utensils:

In addition to the standard galley utensils, there are a few items well worth having in Mexico. The first is a lime press, which we use just about daily. This is a small hand utensil that is sized to hold the small limes common in Mexico. We use ours to squeeze lime juice into beers, when making guacamole or salsa, and to add lime juice to fish or shrimp. Don't bother to buy one in the U.S. because it will be sized for lemons rather than small limes. In Mexico, they are readily available at most larger *tiendas* or *mercados* for 15 to 45 pesos. Lime presses come in plastic or metal, and we have used both. The metal ones seem to work a bit better, but look for one with small holes so that smaller seeds don't get through with the juice. My think-outside-the-box husband figured out that it is easier to squeeze limes if you put them in the press cut side down, although this method sometimes results in more seeds escaping.

One utensil that you may wish to bring with you is a good instant-read thermometer. We find ours invaluable for testing the temperature of water to dissolve yeast when baking, and to check the doneness of meat and fish, especially when grilling. I generally carry a spare on board, since I have killed a couple of good thermometers by thoughtlessly immersing them in dishwater! For a table listing temperatures for properly cooked meat, fish, and poultry, look in Substitutions, Conversions, and Rules of Thumb.

It is also a good idea to have an oven thermometer if you plan to do any baking, and some cruisers invest in a refrigerator thermometer so they can monitor how well their refrigeration is working. One clever idea is to use an indoor/outdoor-style thermometer that has multiple remote sensors. By placing remote sensors in the freezer and the refrigerator, you can monitor the temperature without opening the lid.

Next is a tortilla warmer, another item to buy once you arrive in Mexico. They are commonly available in two types. The first is a hard plastic round container with lid similar to those seen in Mexican restaurants in the U.S. The second looks like an over-sized, round oven mitt. Nice, well-insulated ones are sometimes sold in upscale restaurants decorated with the restaurant logo, or in convenience or gift shops with beer or other logos at a price of 60–100 pesos. You can find flimsier versions for about 20 pesos at Wal-Mart and similar stores. Either type can be used to warm tortillas in the microwave or to keep tortillas warm that have been heated by other methods. Flour tortillas too large to lie flat in the warmer are folded into quarters for heating.

Another utensil that I use almost daily is a garlic press. Many Mexican foods call for garlic and I find it easier to press garlic than to mince it. You can either bring a garlic press with you or buy one inexpensively in Mexico.

One item that we appreciate onboard was an afterthought when we moved from our house onto the boat. A good rolling pin and a flexible Tupperware pastry sheet

Several styles of tortilla warmers are available for purchase in Mexico. Shown in this photo are a hard plastic warmer and an "oven mitt" style warmer.

have come in handy many times. While a wine bottle or thick wooden dowel can be pressed into service as a makeshift rolling pin, I find that by wrapping my pastry sheet around the rolling pin the two items can be stored compactly together. We use them for making pie crust, English muffins, biscuits, and flour tortillas.

Egg containers:

As mentioned previously, egg containers are needed to safely transport eggs from smaller tiendas. I carry two egg containers aboard. The first is a flat rectangular Rubbermaid container that holds 20 eggs and is also useful for taking deviled eggs to a potluck or dinghy raft-up. The other is a compact camping-style carrier that holds a dozen eggs. I take this one to stores with me and also use it for overflow egg storage in the fridge or to segregate hard-boiled eggs from uncooked eggs.

Propane Barbecue:

Most cruising boats in Mexico are equipped with some sort of propane barbecue, which seems to get frequent use. Some cruisers use small disposable propane canisters to fuel their barbecue. While these canisters are available in large stores in Mexico, they are generally expensive. Some cruisers use a special connection to refill their disposable canisters from their main propane tanks. We initially hooked our barbecue to our main propane tanks using a connection on the low pressure side of the system. We found that it was difficult to keep the barbecue lit if I was using the oven or a couple of stove burners. Later, we added a separate small, refillable propane tank dedicated to the barbecue. That solution works well for us.

Pressure cooker—yes or no?

Many books about cruising galleys recommend having a pressure cooker aboard. We do have one on Legacy, but don't use it nearly as much as we expected. The arguments for carrying a pressure cooker include shorter cooking times, which save propane and keep the cabin cooler, and the ability to preserve foods should the refrigeration fail. While we do use our pressure cooker for stews and other slow-cooked foods, we find that those are foods that we don't eat often in Mexico. Instead, we tend to grill or use foods that cook quickly. In Mexico, we're never more than a couple of days from somewhere that ice is available, so food preservation isn't as much of an issue as it would be on a long ocean passage.

Ingredients and Cooking Terms

IN MEXICAN MARKETS AND GROCERY STORES, you will find a wide variety of foods, both familiar and unfamiliar. For better or worse, since NAFTA there are many more U.S. brand foods available in Mexican grocery stores, as well as products from multi-national firms that are familiar to U.S. shoppers. While you will probably be shopping primarily for the foods you normally use in the U.S. or Canada, you will miss part of the joy of traveling in Mexico if you don't try some of the local foods. I make a point of trying one unfamiliar item each time I shop. Since most foods are very inexpensive in Mexico, you won't be out too much money if you don't like what you try.

THE DAIRY CASE:

Butter: *mantequilla* Butter is available in all but some smaller towns. We like the Mexican brand Gloria's which is sold in quarter and half pound bars as well as pound packages of four bars. In larger stores, you can frequently find Fern butter from New Zealand and Lurpak butter from Denmark. Both are excellent.

Cottage Cheese: *queso tipo cottage* Mexican brands are commonly available. If you find U.S. brands, they are likely to be expensive.

Cream: *crema* Crema is a generic term for cream. However, in general usage *crema* means *crema ácida* or sour cream. You will get strange looks in Mexican restaurants if you ask for *café con crema*, rather than *café con leche* (coffee with milk). In the recipes in this book, if I specify *crema*, I mean *crema ácida*. In the refrigerated case, you may find coffee creamers, but not half-and-half (except in large stores on the Baja). In large stores you may find whipping cream *(crema para batir)* which we cut with milk to make our own "half and half" for use in coffee and recipes.

Cream Cheese: *queso crema* Cream cheese is widely available throughout Mexico. You'll find the familiar Philadelphia brand in the silver wrapper, as well as various Mexican brands. In fact in some areas, cream cheese is colloquially known as "Philadelphia!"

Eggs: *huevos* You won't find eggs in the dairy case. In Mexico, eggs are sold unrefrigerated, generally in the produce section. You will find them sold in cartons and flats in larger stores, and loose by the kilo or dozen in smaller stores.

Margarine: *margarina* Cheap Mexican brands of margarine are reportedly pretty bad. In large stores, you may see some U.S. brands, such as "I Can't Believe It's Not Butter."

Milk: *leche* Fresh milk is available in all larger stores and many smaller *tiendas*, and you will also find ultra-pasteurized milk in aseptic packages on the shelf. *Leche entero* is whole milk; 2% reduced fat milk is called Light or *semi descremada*. *Leche Descremada* is usually 1% reduced fat milk; skim milk is rarely seen.

Packaged jello, flan, and pudding: *gelatina, flan, postre* In the dairy case, you'll find a variety of individually packaged puddings and desserts. The ones I've tried aren't bad.

Processed Cheeses: *quesos* As in the U.S. you'll find various processed cheeses in the dairy case (frequently *tipo Chihuahua, tipo Oaxaca, or Amarillo*). Try the deli counter for a better selection of quality fresh bulk cheeses.

Smoothies: *Licuados* In Mexico, you'll find the dairy case full of various milk, yogurt, and fruit beverages sold in individual plastic bottles or larger cartons. Try a few; they're delicious!

Sour Cream: *crema ácida* is found in most stores under brand names such as Lala, Alpura, and Eugenia. Try a couple of different brands until you find one you like. The texture will be somewhat softer and the taste sweeter than U.S. sour cream. You can add a little lime juice or vinegar if you like more tang. If *crema* is called for in a recipe, it means *crema ácida* unless otherwise specified.

Yogurt: *yogurt* You'll find a huge array of yogurt in larger stores, some plain and some with fruit, cereal, or other additions. Some are familiar brands, such as Dannon and Yoplait, but the taste and texture may be different. Try a few to discover which brand you enjoy. In addition to yogurt in a cup, you'll also find yogurt for drinking in small bottles. It is difficult to find unsweetened plain yogurt. Yogurt that is labeled "natural" is generally unflavored, but likely contains sugar.

THE DELI COUNTER:

Lunch meats: *carnes frias* The joke on Legacy is that you can have any type of lunch meat you want as long as it's ham *(jamón)!* You will find many varieties of ham at the deli counter and in smaller *tiendas* as well. Also available, but less common, are turkey breast *(pechuga de pavo)*, salami, and sometimes roast beef *(rosbif)* and pastrami.

Chorizo: *Chorizo* is a spicy sausage, usually soft and contained in a casing. You'll find a bewildering variety at the deli counter under various brands and types. It is excellent in *paella* or cooked with scrambled eggs for breakfast or lunch.

Hot Dogs: *salchichas* Zwan hot dogs are generally better than FUD, but Oscar Meyer or Ballpark hot dogs are also found at times. Mexican brands are frequently made of turkey or chicken.

Roasted Chicken: *pollo rostizada* Roasted chickens are sold in most larger stores, as well as in small storefronts or take-out restaurants in just about every town. When provisioning, I buy one or two chickens, pull the meat from the bones, and freeze the cooked chicken in meal-size pouches for use in quesadillas, sandwiches, or salads.

Other: Sometimes deli counters will have tamales, *mole* or other chile sauces by the cup, and puddings or other desserts.

CHEESES:

At the deli counter, you will usually find a large display of cheeses, which are an important part of the Mexican diet. Most are white, not yellow or orange. The attendant behind the counter will give you a sample if you wish. Just say *"Quiero probarlo* (I want to try it)."* Although you will see imported cheeses, generally expensive, in some large stores, I'm going to focus on the Mexican cheeses you will see. They are divided below into melting cheeses, fresh cheeses, and hard cheeses.

> ### The Best Hot Dogs in the Sea of Cortez:
>
> In sleepy little Santa Rosalia, you'll find the best hot dogs in the Sea of Cortez. After 6 p.m., the hot dog vendor, Hot Dogs Chuyita, sets up on the street between the city square and the Eiffel church. Ignore your cholesterol count for the evening, order a hot dog or two with everything (*con todo*) and settle down on a park bench to enjoy this messy treat. The hot dogs taste so good because the vendor wraps them in bacon and fries them!

Melting Cheeses:

Asadero: This is a classic cheese for quesadillas. It is semisoft, mellow, and buttery and can be used as a substitute for cheddar, Muenster, Monterey Jack, or provolone. Sometimes clerks at the cheese counter will refer to asadero as "cheddar".

Chihuahua: This is one of the most commonly seen cheeses and is often available in many different variations. You may also see it named *"queso menonito"* as it was introduced by Mennonite immigrants, who still live and farm in the State of Chihuahua. This pale cheese tastes like a mild cheddar or a tangy jack, and is good for tacos, enchiladas, and grilled cheese sandwiches.

Manchego: This cheese is often golden-colored with smooth texture and a medium taste. It melts easily for use in quesadillas, nachos, and sandwiches. *Manchego* is often sold sliced for sandwiches.

Oaxaca: This is a white cheese, frequently sold in woven balls. It is similar to string cheese and makes a good substitute for mozzarella though processed *tipo* or *imitation* Oaxaca found in some stores may not melt quite as well. Use on pizzas, in fondues, or in quesadillas or nachos.

Cheeses, eggs, and refrigerated items are sold at this *mercado* stall. The owner will cut samples of the different cheeses so you can decide which one you like.

Fresh Cheeses:

Cuajada: This is a fresh cheese with mild flavor that is excellent with fruit.

Panela: This cheese has a texture like fresh mozzarella and is usually fairly mild in taste. It can be cubed or sliced for sandwiches, salads, or soups. Slices can be pan browned.

Queso fresco: This is a soft, moist cheese similar to farmer's cheese, which is mildly salty and crumbles easily for use on enchiladas, beans, and vegetables.

Requeson: This soft, milky cheese is similar to ricotta and can be used in lasagna, enchiladas, or desserts.

Hard Cheeses:

Anejo: This hard, white cheese is dry, sharp, and salty. It can be grated and used as a substitute for Romano or parmesan.

Cotija: This is a sharp, tangy, and crumbly cheese. It can be used like feta, parmesan, or Romano.

Enchilado: The surface of this cheese is coated with a mild red chile paste that adds a slight note of spiciness. It is excellent sliced or cubed for eating, or crumbled onto salads, soups, or pastas.

MEATS:

The ability to shop for meat in the *carnecería* section of a large Mexican *mercado* is the sign of a true carnivore! I don't like to be on a first-name basis with my meat, so usually shop for meat in large stores or specialty markets catering to gringos. Most Mexican cuts of meat are very thin, designed to cook quickly. You will frequently see thicker chops or steaks labeled *"americano"*.

Types of meat:

Bacon: *tocino* Mexican bacon is delicious. Sliced bacon is *tocino rebanado.*
   Beef: *res, carne de res* Mexican beef is frequently disappointing to travelers from the U.S. and Canada because most of it is not aged and sometimes tough. If you want tender, American-style steaks, your best bet is to buy beef in specialty markets that cater to gringos and tourist restaurants. Sonoran beef is highly valued for its taste and texture. *Arrachera* is thin flank steak that has been tenderized and, frequently, marinated.
   Goat: *cabrito* or *chivo*
   Ham: *jamón* Usually refers to pressed ham.

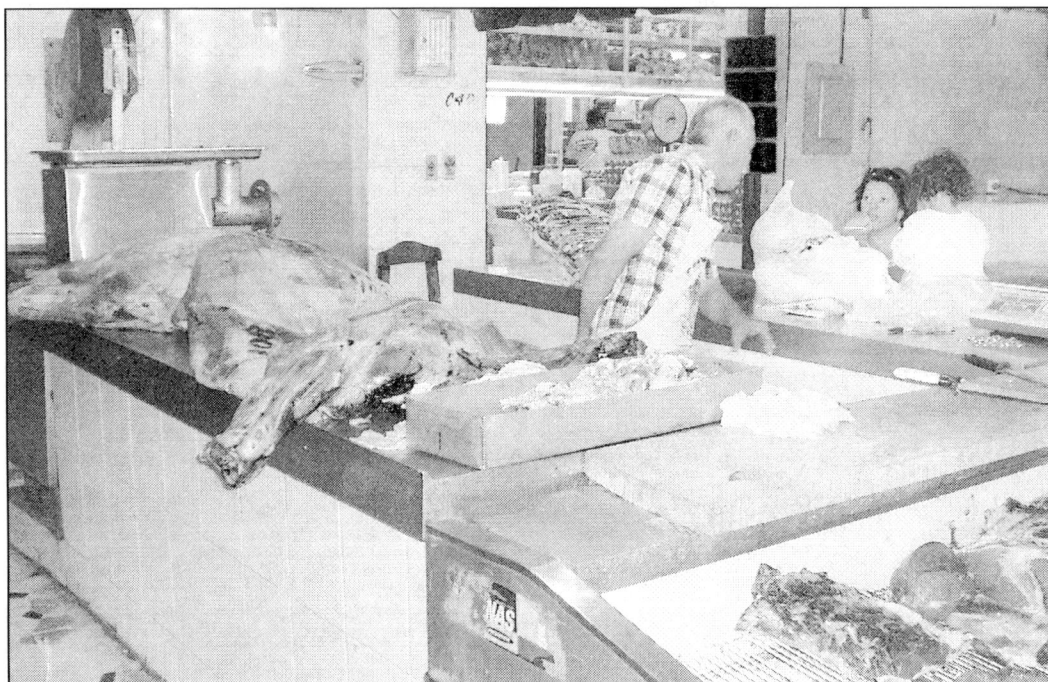

A side of beef rests on a counter in the *mercado* in preparation for butchering and sale. Beef is not usually aged in Mexico, so the meat is not always as tender as *gringos* expect.

Lamb: *borrego or carnero* May only be available in the spring except at markets or restaurants that specialize in lamb.

Organ meats: At the *carnecería* and the grocery store, you can buy just about every part of the animal, including liver *(hígado)*, heart *(corazón)*, tongue *(lengua)*, kidneys *(riñones)*, brains *(sesos)*, and tripe *(tripas)*.

Pork: *puerco, carne de puerco* Mexican pork is very good and inexpensive.

Veal: *ternero*

Venison: *venado*

Cuts of meat:

If you want a piece of meat whole instead of cut into pieces, make sure you specify "*entero*" or "*pedazo entero*".

Bones: *huesos*

Chops: *chuleta* Most chops will be very thin, unless you have them cut to order. When available, thick cut chops may be labeled *chuleta Americano*.

Ground meat: *carne molida* At specialty meat markets, you may be able to specify either straight meat or a percentage of meat and fat (80% meat, 20% fat is typical). To get finely ground hamburger meat, request *carne de res doble molida* (beef ground twice).

Ribs: *costillas*

Roast: *trozo* or *rosbif* Roasts are not a cut commonly used in Mexico. Your best bet is to find a butcher in a specialty meat market who understands *gringo* cuts.

Steak: *bistec or filete* Mexican-style steaks will generally be pounded flat to tenderize *(aplanada)*. If you want a thick, American style steak, look for NY strip, ribeye steak, or filet in a large store or specialty market. Frequently specialty markets will sell you a whole filet that you can have cut into steaks of your preferred thickness.

Stew meat: *carne para caldo* or *pulpa*

Tenderloin: *lomo* or *filete*

POULTRY:

Chicken: *pollo* Mexican chicken is plentiful, flavorful, and inexpensive. Most stores have chicken in some form. Large stores will have whole chickens *(pollo entero)*, roasted chickens *(pollo rostizada)*, chicken breast *(pechuga de pollo)*, chicken thighs *(muslo de pollo)*, drumsticks *(peirna de pollo)*, and boneless breast and thigh *(sin huesos)*. Poultry counters in the central mercado will have piles of chicken feet and maybe heads. Some Mexican chicken has a beautiful golden color resulting from being fed marigold flowers.

Game hens: *pollito tierno* Are sometimes seen in the freezer case of large stores.

Turkey: *pavo or guajolote* Less frequently seen, but frozen turkeys are sold in some large stores and specialty meat markets, especially around the holiday season.

SEAFOOD:

Seafood is very popular everywhere in Mexico and you can buy it in many places: grocery stores large and small, specialty fish markets *(pescadería)*, from the docks serving

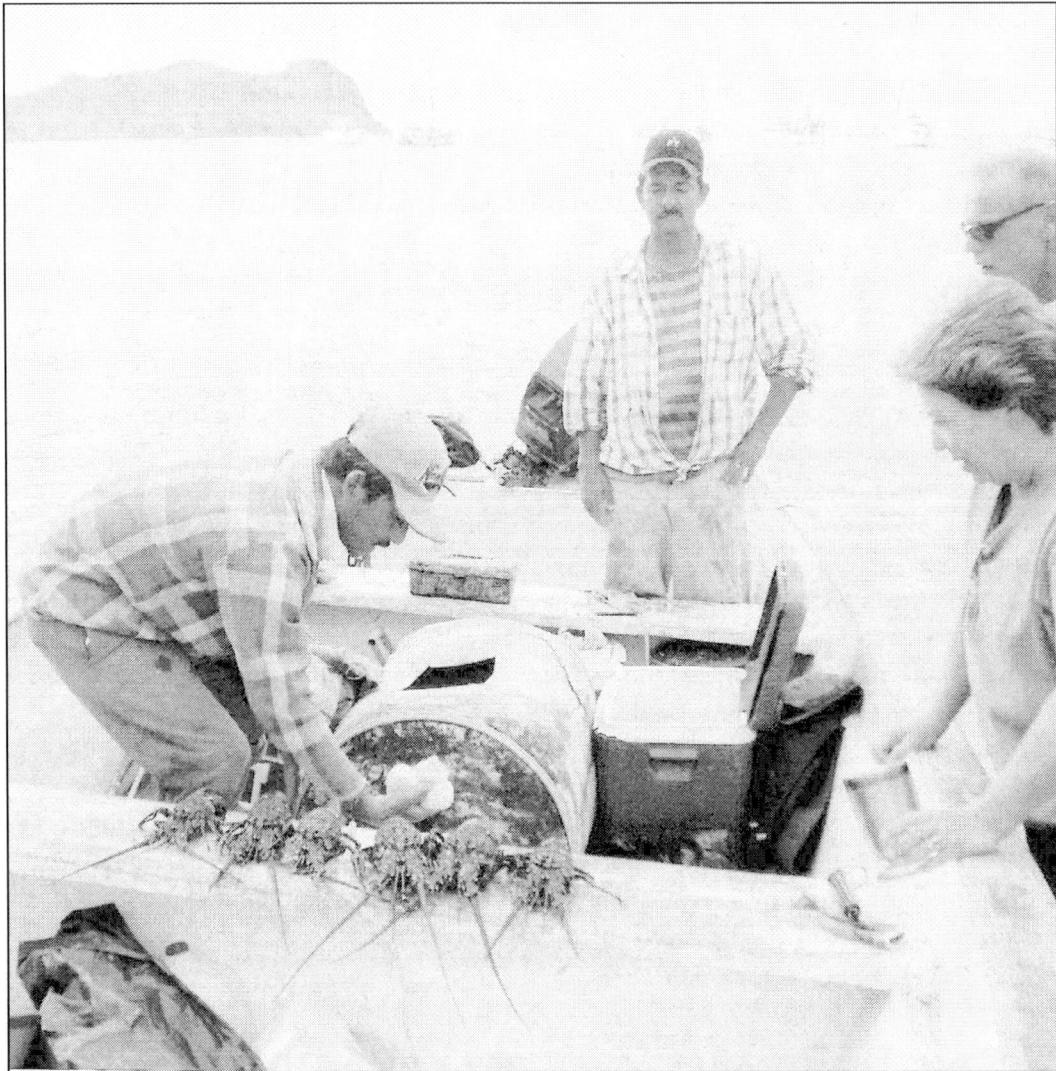

These enterprising *pangueros* stopped by a beach in Agua Verde where cruisers were gathered for a potluck. In short order, they managed to sell most of their catch of lobsters and scallops. (Joan Stockard photo)

fishing boats, and from vendors with trucks or just coolers. Most large stores have a seafood *(mariscos)* counter. In small villages, fisherman in *pangas* may offer fish they have caught that day or take orders for fish or lobster caught to order.

Bass: *lobina*

Clams: *almejas* Along the Baja you will encounter *chocolates*, a tasty large clam great in chowders and stews, and the tiny butter clam, which is delicious steamed.

Conch: *caracol*

Crab: *cangrejo*

Fish: *pescado* A live fish is a *pez*; a whole fish is *pescado entero*, and filets are *filetes*. The type of fish may or not be specified, and it may not mean anything to you if it is specified. Menus or fish markets frequently offer generic white fish *(pescado blanco* or *filetes blanco)*.

Grouper: *mero*

Lobster: *langosta*

Mackeral: *sierra* Sierra is commonly used in *ceviche* and is delicious to eat.

Octopus: *pulpo*

Oysters: *ostiones*

Red Snapper: *huachinango* Red snapper is frequently served in restaurants, and is often served whole.

Sardines: *sardines*

Scallops: *callos*

Sea Bass: *robalo*

Shrimp: *camarones* Shrimp in Mexico are wonderful and found everywhere. If you are buying shrimp direct from a fisherman or vendor, make sure you know whether the quoted price per kilo is for shrimps with heads *(con cabeza)* or without *(sin cabeza)*.

Squid: *calamares*

Tuna: *atún* Tuna is sold both fresh and canned.

Yellowtail: *jurel*

Other types of fish you may catch or buy include *dorado* (mahi-mahi), *wahoo*, and marlin.

FROZEN FOODS:

The freezer cases, even in large stores, will be much smaller than in the U.S. and Canada. The selection of frozen foods is quite limited.

Ice Cream: *helado* Most of the freezer case will be devoted to ice cream, which is extremely popular in Mexico. Common brands are Nestle and Holanda. Whether from the grocery store or one of the many ice cream shops, try some of the wonderful and exotic flavors of Mexican ice cream. Flavors we've seen include tamarind, coconut, pistachio, tequila-almond, grape, and mango. Vanilla is much more intensely flavored than in other parts of North America.

Prepared Foods: The selection of frozen prepared foods is small. You may see fish sticks, chicken fingers, *flautas, taquitos*, pizza, waffles, pancakes, and sometimes bagels.

Fruits and Vegetables: Most larger stores will have a small selection of frozen fruits and vegetables, including strawberries, corn, spinach, French fries, and mixed vegetables. Some stores have frozen peas or green beans. We've seen bags of frozen mangoes at Sam's Club.

PRODUCE:

Coming from Alaska, I was in heaven when I first encountered Mexican produce. Items are excellent and mostly dirt cheap. For example, you will find grapefruit and oranges for 4–5 pesos per kilo. The most expensive items, such as avocados and red and yellow bell peppers, may be 22–35 pesos per kilo,but that is still much cheaper than comparable items in the U.S.

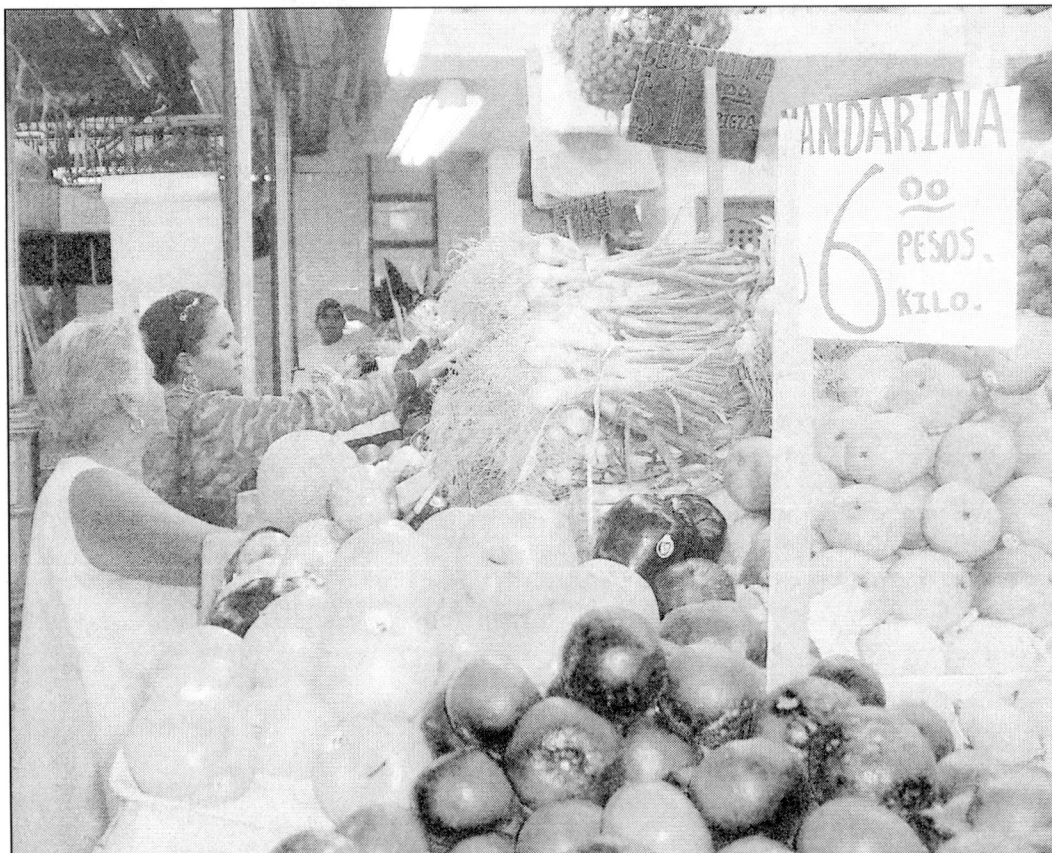

Fruits and vegetables heaped in a *mercado* stall make a bountiful display. When I arrive at the *mercado*, I stroll through first to identify which stalls I think have the nicest goods.

Apples: *manzanas* Many of the apples you find in the produce section come from the U.S., however there is a large apple-growing region in the Mexican state of Chihuahua.

Apricots: *chabacanos*

Artichokes: *alcachofas* You will sometimes find fresh artichokes in larger stores, but they are more commonly found in cans or jars. Occasionally, you can find a wonderful artichoke relish that makes a great appetizer spread on crackers or crostini.

Asparagus: *espárrago*

Avocado: *aguacate* I've been spoiled by Mexican avocados. I enjoy always having them on hand for salads or guacamole and use them only when they are perfectly ripe. Quite a change from Alaska where I rarely encountered a ripe avocado! Avocados are frequently hard to find in smaller towns, especially on the Baja.

Banana: *plátano* or *banana* Tiny bananas are frequently called *plátano domingo*, and they are deliciously sweet.

Basil: *albahaca* or *albahacar*

Beets: *betabeles*

Bell Pepper: *pimienta, pimienta dulce*

Broccoli: *brécol* or *brócoli* Broccoli and cauliflower are more frequently seen in the cooler, northern regions of the Mexican mainland.

Brussels sprouts: *col de bruselas*

Cabbage: *col* or *repello* In addition to green cabbage, you will also see red cabbage, which is called *col morado*.

Cactus: *nopales, nopalitos* Stores offering *nopales* cactus will frequently have a woman behind a portable counter pulling spikes out of the cactus, splitting the leaves, and dicing the meat. We enjoy cactus salad and generally buy fresh, diced *nopales* for that use.

Canteloupe: *melón* The word *melón* is used for all types of melon except watermelon. Canteloupe in Mexico is wonderful, especially during the spring harvest season. Make sure to scrub the outside of cantaloupes with soap and water before cutting into them to avoid contamination.

Carrot: *zanahoria* Carrots are plentiful and cheap in Mexico but they tend to be shorter and fatter than U.S. carrots. *Zanahoria* is one of my favorite Spanish words because of the way it rolls off my tongue.

Cauliflower: *coliflor*

Celery: *apio*

Chayote: *chayote* is a vegetable that looks like a hairy squash and is frequently served steamed or sautéed.

Cherries: *cerezas*

Chiles: *Chiles* are sold everywhere, and many varieties are found in larger stores. Popular types are very mild *poblano* chiles (which are used for *chiles rellenos*), jalapeño, *serrano, ancho, chipotle,* and *habanero*.

Cilantro: *cilantro* Fresh cilantro is used heavily in Mexican cooking and is available very inexpensively in all but the smallest *tiendas*. If you don't see cilantro in a small *tienda*, ask because they may have it refrigerated rather than on display.

Coconut: *coco* While *cocos* are sold in grocery stores, you will often see cold *cocos* sold at roadside stands. The vendor will whack off the top with a machete and serve it to you with a straw for drinking the cold coconut water inside. After the liquid is gone, the vendor will hack up the shell and remove the coconut meat for you.

Corn on the cob: *elotes* Mexican corn on the cob is very tasty, but less tender than U.S. sweet corn. Street vendors will frequently offer roasted *elotes* with lime juice and chile powder, a popular Mexican snack.

Cucumber: *pepino*

Eggplant: *berenjena*

Eggs: *huevos* In Mexico, eggs are sold unrefrigerated, usually in the produce section. Larger stores will offer eggs in 12 or 18 egg cartons, as well as bulk eggs sold by the kilo. Smaller stores may have only bulk eggs.

Figs: *higos*

Fruits: *frutas* Some of the exotic fruits you may see are *chirimoya* (greenish fruit with white inner pulp), *mamey* (oval-shaped fruit with bumpy brown skin and purplish pulp), *tuna* (the fruit of the nopal cactus), *tamarind* (looks like a large brown pod), and *guayaba* (guava).

A vendor uses a machete to open *cocos* for drinking. After the customer finishes drinking the water inside, the vendor will chop out the coconut meat and put it in a bag for the customer to take home.

Garlic: *ajo* Garlic is almost essential in Mexican cooking and is available in just about every *tienda*. In tourist areas or mercados, you may see *ristras*, or braided chains of garlic.

Ginger: *jengibre* Fresh ginger can be found in some large stores.

Grapefruit: *toronja* Grapefruit is plentiful and cheap in the fall and winter months.

Grapes: *uvas* These are least expensive during the late summer and fall harvest season.

Green Beans: *ejotes*

Herbs: *hierbas, yerbas* Fresh herbs can be found in some *mercados* and in large stores. Dried herbs are sold in most grocery stores.

Hibiscus: *Jamaica* Dried hibiscus flowers are sold in packages or bulk in many stores and *mercados*. Hibiscus makes a refreshing tea or *agua fresca* that is a nice substitute for cranberry juice.

Jicama: *jicama* This root vegetable is excellent served raw and makes a reasonable substitute for water chestnuts. Street vendors offer it sprinkled with lime juice, chili powder, and salt.

Leek: *puerro* or *poro*

Lemon: *lima* The whole lemon/lime thing is very confusing in Mexico. You will rarely find yellow lemons in Mexico. The citrus called *lima* looks like a cross between limes sold in the U.S. and a green tangerine.

Lettuce: *lechuga* Large stores sometimes have the tripled-washed bagged lettuce and salads sold in the U.S. Romaine is called *lechuga romana*. I prefer to use the triple-washed lettuce when available to avoid using lots of water to clean and disinfect unwashed heads of lettuce.

Lime: *limón* Most commonly you will see the small round *limónes agria* that are either green or yellow. Limes are extremely cheap and used in just about everything from beer to tacos. *Limónes sin semillas* are larger, more expensive, seedless, and have a less assertive taste than *limones agria*.

Mango: *mango* Mangoes are delicious, juicy, and a mess to eat! The best way I've seen them served is by street vendors who drill a hole in the base, pound in a wooden dowel, peel the mango, then score the flesh to make it easy to eat. Recently we've added an Oxxo Mango Splitter to our galley. This utensil makes it much easier to separate mango flesh from the pit for serving. Frozen mangoes are sometimes available in large markets or "big box" stores.

Melon: *melón* See Cantaloupe.

Mushrooms: *champiñones* Mushrooms are generally fairly expensive and are often sold in plastic-wrapped packages imported from the U.S.

Onion: *cebolla* White onions can be found almost everywhere and red onions are also common. Yellow onions are less frequently available.

Oranges: *naranjas* Oranges in Mexico are rarely a bright orange color as they haven't been dyed like oranges sold in the U.S. *Naranjas para jugo* are very juicy oranges sold for squeezing. Larger stores and some veggie trucks may offer fresh-squeezed orange or tangerine *(mandarina)* juice in plastic jugs.

Papaya: *papaya* Mexican papayas are much larger than the familiar Hawaiian papayas found in U.S. markets. The flesh of Mexican papayas is flavorful, but mealier than Hawaiian papayas. At times, you may find Hawaiian-style papayas, which are sold under the name *papaya cubana*.

Parsley: *perejil* or *peregil*

Peach: *durazno*

Pear: *pera*

Peas: *chícharos*

Peppers: *pimientas* or *chile Morrón* Bell peppers are commonly found in green, red, and yellow colors. Red peppers are called *chile Morrón*.

Pineapple: *piña* Mexican pineapples are sweet and delicious. You may also see *piña dorado*, or golden pineapple which is smaller and sweeter than a standard pineapple.

Plum: *ciruela*

Pomegranate: *granada*

Potatoes: *papas* White-skinned potatoes are found just about everywhere. Russets and red potatoes are less commonly available.

Pumpkin: *calabaza*

Radish: *rábano*

Spinach: *espinaca* Larger stores may have triple-washed bagged spinach.

Squash: *calabaza* or *calabacitas* We like the small *calabacitas* (sometimes known as *calabacita italiana*) that look like little zucchinis.

Squash Flowers: *flores de calabaza* You will see canned squash flowers on the shelf and, occasionally, fresh ones in the produce section. We enjoy fresh squash blossoms fried and added to tacos for a crispy texture. Dip them in milk, dust with cornmeal, then fry in oil. Squash blossoms are also used in soup.

Strawberries: *fresas* Strawberries are plentiful and tasty.

Sweet potato: *camote* may be either yellow or purple.

Tangerine: *mandarina* Tangerines are most common and inexpensive around Christmas.

Tomatoes: *tomates* Both large slicing tomatoes and smaller salad tomatoes are commonly available.

Tomatillos: *tomatillos* or *tomates verde* are small, green tomatoes with a leafy membrane. They are used for chile verde and other sauces.

Turnip: *nabo*

Vegetables: *verduras* or *legumbres*

Watermelon: *sandía* Watermelons are very popular in Mexico. Street vendors may offer cups filled with chunks of watermelon or other fruits.

Yam: *camote* May be yellow or purple.

Zucchini: *calabacitas* The best zucchini are the tiny ones, harvested when they are less than 6 inches long.

BAKED GOODS AND TORTILLAS:

Bread: *pan* Store-bought sandwich bread is pretty bland. The brands most frequently seen are Bimbo and Wonder, both of which have a squishy texture and a very long shelf life. The whole wheat versions (*pan integral, pan multigrano*) are marginally better, and *multigrano linaza* (multigrain with seeds and whole grains) is quite good. Occasionally you may see a multi-seed sandwich bread, either in the refrigerator case or in the *panadería*. Many large markets and *panaderías* also sell baguettes.

Bread rolls: *bolillos* These French-style rolls are very common, inexpensive, and delicious. Like most bread (except supermarket sandwich bread), they are unpreserved and get stale rapidly. They are good for sandwiches and also split and toasted for breakfast. Many veggie trucks sell *bolillos*.

Sweet rolls: *pan dulce* At the *panadería*, you will see a wide variety of *pan dulce*. These rolls are frequently less sweet than similar items in the U.S. and Canada. In addition to traditional types of rolls, most stores also sell crescent rolls, cinnamon rolls, doughnuts, muffins, and cookies *(galletas)*.

Tortillas: *Tortillas* come in corn *(tortillas de maíz)* or flour *(tortillas de harina)*. Flour tortillas are more common on the Baja Peninsula and in the northern parts of the Mexican mainland. Although we generally prefer flour tortillas, a fresh corn tortilla hot off the griddle is a wonderful thing. We eat almost any type of food folded into a tortilla. Every town has one or more *tortillerías*, and many large stores make tortillas on site. Frequently *tortillerías* will make flour tortillas or corn tortillas, but not both. In restaurants, the waiter will ask if you want flour or corn tortillas *(¿harina o maíz?)*. Don't hesitate to ask the waiter for more tortillas if you run out.

> ## Don't get caught with your tortilla inside out!
>
> Which side of the tortilla is the inside? At first glance, both sides of a flour tortilla look identical. If you take a close look, however, you'll see that one side is much thinner than the other. This thin side, called the *pancita* or belly, is the inside. When wrapping a tortilla around food, the *pancita* faces the food. The thicker outside of the tortilla, the back or *espalda*, is less likely to crack or flake.

CANNED GOODS:

Baby food: *alimento infantil* American brands are sold in grocery stores and drug stores *(farmacias)*.

Beans: *frijoles* Canned beans can be either refried beans *(frijoles refrito)* or whole beans *(frijoles entero)*. Black beans are *frijoles negro*, and kidney beans are *bayos*.

Broth: *caldo* Canned chicken or other broth is difficult to find and expensive, however powdered or cubed chicken, tomato, and vegetable broth are readily available. Beef bouillon is less common.

Chiles, salsas, and hot sauces: A tremendous array of salsas, chiles, and hot sauces are sold in just about every store, however mild green chiles like those sold in the U.S. are nearly unavailable. Canned chiles include *jalapeño*, *serrano*, and *chipotle* (smoked jalapeños). Hot sauces are known as *salsa picante*. I like to keep small cans of various salsas on hand for times when I need to add a little kick to a dish. We also keep on hand small jars of *mole* paste to make a quick and delicious chicken *mole*.

Fruits: *frutas* Canned fruits available include peaches, fruit cocktail, and pineapple (slices or chunks, but not crushed).

Jams and jellies: *mermeladas* Strawberry, pineapple, orange, and apricot are common flavors.

Meats: *carnes* You will find few canned meats except for a few processed meats such as Spam, *chilorio*, pate, and deviled chicken or turkey *(jamón del Diablo—pollo o pavo)*.

Chilorio is a mildly spicy, seasoned pork product that we like to keep on hand for quick dinners. It is wonderful scrambled with eggs or served alone in tacos.

Milk products: Ultrapasteurized milk *(leche)* is available in liters and, less commonly, 250 ml aseptic boxes and is quite good. In cans, you will also find evaporated milk *(leche evaporada)*, sweetened condensed milk *(la lechera)*, and *media crema*. We keep *media crema* on hand to make easy sauces to go with fish or poultry. You will also find powdered milk in many stores. Nido is a popular brand.

Pasta and pizza sauces: Most larger markets have canned pasta and pizza sauce, frequently Ragu brand.

Prepared foods: Except for the prepared meats noted above, you won't find many prepared foods on the shelf. Mexican cooks more frequently use a canned sauce to prepare fresh meat or poultry. For instant meals, you will see Maruchan Instant Lunch and Cup of Noodles.

Seafood: Canned seafood is very popular and found in even the smallest *tiendas*. Tuna *(atún)* is very common. You may also see sardines *(sardinas)*, clams *(almejas)*, and shrimp *(camarones)*.

Soups: *sopas* In the soup aisle, you'll see the familiar red and white labels of Campbell's soups, but the flavors are quite different from those sold in the U.S. and Canada. Even common tomato soup has slightly different seasoning to appeal to the Latin American market. Try some of the unusual flavors, which can be quite delicious. We especially enjoy *flor de calabasa* or squash blossom soup. In addition to canned soups, you'll find a variety of dried soup packets.

Vegetables: *verduras* or *legumbres* In cans or aseptic boxes, you will find mushrooms, peas & carrots, peas, corn, and cubed potatoes.

STAPLES AND DRY GOODS:

Baking Powder: *polvo para hornear* Most common brand is Royal.

Baking Soda: *Bicarbonato sódico* Arm & Hammer is common.

Brown Sugar: Except in stores catering to *gringos*, you probably won't see boxed brown sugar on the shelf. Instead, go to the produce section and look for hard cones or chunks of dark brown sugar called *piloncillo*. I use this by grating the hard sugar, then lightly pressing it into a cup or spoon to measure.

Cocoa and chocolate: Hershey's cocoa is sometimes available, but expensive. For eating chocolate, both U.S. brands and Mexican brands (King Carlos V, Larín) are available in large stores. For baking chocolate, try the excellent Turin brand. You will see milk chocolate *(chocolate con leche)*, semisweet *(semi amargo)*, and bittersweet *(amargo)*. Chocolate chips are difficult to find and expensive. Mexican drinking chocolate is wonderful, sold under the brands *Ibarra* or *Abuelita*.

Corn Starch: *maizena*

Corn Syrup: *jarabe de maíz* Corn syrup is frequently labeled for use sweetening baby foods.

Cornmeal: *harina de maíz amarilla*

Dried beans: *frijol* Note that uncooked beans are called *frijol* and cooked beans are *frijoles*. You will find a wide variety of dried beans in most stores. Don't buy the cheapest brand as they may be old or of poor quality. Wash dried beans carefully and watch for small stones.

Dried Fruits: Specialty stores and *mercado* stalls may have many varieties of dried fruits, including papaya, mango, and pineapple. In the grocery store, you will probably see prunes *(ciruela pasa)* and raisins *(uva pasa)* although it's frequently hard to figure out where they are shelved in the store.

Flour: *harina* White flour is *harina de trigo*, and whole wheat flour is *harina de trigo integral*.

Honey: *miel de abeja* Honey can be found prepackaged in most stores, and local honey is available throughout Mexico. It may be sold in a container or in bulk. Note that *miel* is a general term for honey, molasses, and syrups.

Molasses: *miel de sorgo* or *melaza* Molasses is very hard to find in most areas frequented by cruisers.

Nuts: *nuez* (plural is *nueces*) Peanuts *(cacahuates)* are very popular and can be found anywhere. Pecans *(nuez)* and almonds *(almendra)* are available but may be expensive. Walnuts are rare. Cashews *(nuez de India or marañon)* are sometimes available. Some large stores carry the same large jars of Kirkland brand cashews, mixed nuts, and peanuts that you can find at Costco.

Oatmeal and cereals: Oatmeal is *avena* and you may find Quaker Oats. Dried cereals are widely available and frequently known by their English names. Corn flakes are the most common cereal, but you may also see Cheerios, Corn Pops, Special K, Trix, Raisin Bran, and others.

Pastas: *macarrones, spaghetti, fideos, pasta* Most stores carry a variety of pastas including both U.S. and Mexican brands. Some of the cheaper Mexican brands are softer and get soggy easily or clump together and never get done no matter how long they are boiled.

Pudding and gelatin mixes: *Flan* mix is readily available in Mexican stores, however other pudding mixes are generally not available. Those cruisers that like to have instant pudding mixes aboard generally bring them from the U.S. Gelatin mixes are commonly available.

Rice: *arroz* When buying rice, avoid the cheaper types which may be old or dirty. While lots of brands of rice are available, there is little variety when it comes to types of rice. If you like specialty rices such as Asian rice, basmati, or Jasmine, bring them with you as they are hard to find.

Shortening: *manteca vegetal* A common brand is Cristal. Crisco shortening can be found in a few stores catering to gringos.

Sugar: *azúcar* Common Mexican brands of sugar *(azúcar estándar)* range from light brown and a bit coarser than U.S. granulated sugar to a product that is nearly identical to U.S. brands. You may also find *azúcar refinada*, which is white and finely-textured like U.S. sugar. Some larger markets sell *azúcar glass*, which is similar to U.S. confectioner's or powdered sugar.

Yeast: *levadura* Yeast is generally sold in large bags. Occasionally, you'll see the familiar individual envelopes or small jars, but they are quite expensive. For the amount of baking I do, one 4–ounce jar brought from the U.S. will last the season.

OIL, VINEGAR, CONDIMENTS, SPICES, AND SEASONINGS:

Catsup: *salsa de tomate catsup* Heinz, Hunt's, and Del Monte are often available.

Mayonnaise: *mayonesa* Hellman's and McCormick's are commonly available. Some Hellman's mayonnaise sold in Mexico is flavored with lime juice *(con jugo de limón)*, so pay attention to the labels.

Mustard: *mostaza* Yellow mustard is common, including French's and McCormick's. Large stores may have good brands of imported mustard.

Oil: *aceite comestible* Olive oil *(aceite de oliva)*, canola oil *(aceite de canola)*, and safflower oil *(aceite de cartamo)* are widely available. Sesame oil *(aceite de ajonjolí)* may be available, particularly in specialty stores.

Pickles and Pickle Relish: *pepinos* Sweet pickles *(pepinos dulces)*, dill pickles *(pepinos agrios)*, and pickle relish *(picados aderazados)* can be found in large stores.

Salad Dressing: *aderezo para ensaladas* The selection of bottled salad dressings is limited, even in large stores, but may include Italian, Ranch, Thousand Island, and Caesar.

Salt: *sal*

Soy Sauce: *salsa soya*

Spices: *especias*

Vanilla: *vainilla* Mexico is justifiably famous for its vanilla. It is plentiful and cheap in even the smallest markets, and in tourist areas you can find large bottles that make nice presents for folks back home. Most vanilla-flavored items in Mexico have a much more intense vanilla taste than *norteamericanos* are used to.

Vinegar: *vinagre* White and cider vinegars are common. Large markets may also have red and white wine vinegar and balsamic vinegar.

Worchestershire sauce: *salsa inglesa*

SNACKS, COOKIES, AND CRACKERS:

Candy: *dulce* In addition to U.S. and other imported candies, stores carry a variety of very interesting regional sweets, many of them made from fruit. We're particularly fond of various coconut candies, as well as a milk-based sweet called *jamoncillo*. Caramel *(cajeta)* is very popular and caramel syrup is sold in almost every store. A favorite Mexican snack is caramel on a saltine cracker. The most flavorful *cajeta* is made of goat's milk *(leche de cabrito)*.

Cookies: *galletas* On the cookie aisle, you'll find some common U.S. brands such as Oreos and Chips Ahoy. You will also see some interesting and delicious Mexican

---

> **Familiar brands; unfamiliar flavors:**
>
> On the cookie aisle, you'll find familiar Oreos, but in different flavors than in the U.S. We particularly like the Oreos stuffed with cinnamon and vanilla *(canela y vainilla)* or with chocolate and strawberry *(ChocoFresa)*. Mint crème is red rather than green. Trying the different varieties produced for the Latin America market is a fun way to sample the "flavor" of the country!

brands. We like Emperadors (sandwich cookies) and Suavi-cremas (wafer cookies). Also interesting are Florentines, which are shortbread-like cookies filled with fruit or caramel.

Crackers: *galletas saladas* Mexicans eat a lot of crackers and are especially fond of saltines *(saltines)*. Ritz crackers and a Mexican copy *(Crackets)* are available in most stores. *Pan cremas* are similar to U.S. club crackers. Other snack crackers are rare.

Marshmallows: *malvaviscos* Marshmallows are commonly available, and miniature marshmallows can be found in some larger markets.

Peanuts: *cacahuates* Peanuts are another very popular snack and are sold both plain and with spicy seasonings.

Popcorn: *maíz palomero* Microwave popcorn is sold in every *tienda*. Some convenience stores will pop it for you.

Potato Chips: *papas fritas* They come both plain and in interesting flavors. Many stores carry Pringles potato crisps.

Tortilla Chips: *totopes* Some brands are quite tasty; others are rather bland. Try a few and find a brand you like. Large stores carry Doritos in a variety of flavors.

> ### Strange Cravings:
>
> At times we've found that we have strange cravings for items we never eat in the U.S. For example, at one potluck we attended, a cruiser brought a bag of Cheetos as his contribution. Cruisers attacked the bag like it was the most delectable gourmet treat they had ever seen. We found that the next time we saw Cheetos in the market, we just had to have a bag!

NONALCOHOLIC BEVERAGES:

Beverage Mixes: Most stores have a variety of beverage mixes. Many cruisers like *Clight*, which is a Mexican version of artificially-sweetened Crystal Light. Our favorite flavors are limeade *(limonada)*, pink grapefruit *(toronja rosada)*, pineapple coconut *(piña colada)*, and hibiscus *(Jamaica)*. Tang is also commonly available. Powdered Gatorade is occasionally found in large stores, and bottled Gatorade is sold everywhere.

Bottled Water: *agua embotellada* is sold everywhere.

Coffee: *café* Most stores carry coffee, ground or whole bean. Make sure you look at it carefully because Mexican coffee frequently contains sugar. For American-style coffee, look for *café sin azúcar* or *café estilo Americano*. We like *Café Combaté* or *Café Garat*. In some areas, you will also find excellent locally roasted brands such as Evie's Coffee in San Carlos. Coffee is much cheaper than in the U.S.

Fruit Juices: *jugos* Fruit juice is usually sold in aseptic boxes in liter and 250 ml sizes. Try some of the more interesting varieties such as *mango, guayaba* (guava), and *papaya*.

Soda: *refresco* Coke and Pepsi products are common in both sugared and diet versions. Mexican brands include Toni-Cal, and a variety of fruit-flavored sodas.

Tea: *té* Black tea is *té negro*.

Tonic Water: *agua mineral de manantial quinada, quinac, or agua quinada* Commonly found in sugared, but not diet versions. The most common brand is *Peñafiel*.

BEER, WINE, AND LIQUOR:

Beer, rum, tequila, and brandy are sold in most tiendas. Large grocery stores will also have a variety of wines and other liquors. For a variety of U.S. liquors, your best bet will be a large liquor store *(licorerías or vinos y licores)*.

Beer: *cerveza* Beer is available just about everywhere. Pacifico, Corona, and Modelo are common brands. Cans are considered higher class as bottled beer is much cheaper. If you have bottles to turn in, you'll avoid paying the deposit. Generally, the cheapest place to buy beer is the *Deposito*, which is an agent for the beer manufacturer.

Brandy: Is very popular in Mexico.

Kahlua: Since it is made in Mexico, Kahlua is quite inexpensive and available in most *tiendas*.

Rum: *ron* Plentiful and cheap.

Tequila: Tequilas range from cheap rotgut to wonderful aged sipping tequilas, and the prices generally reflect the difference.

Vermouth: *vermut* Handy to have on board to substitute for white wine in recipes if you don't have a bottle open. Martini is about the only brand you'll see.

Wine: Supermarket brands of wine can be pretty awful, although many cruisers like the "California" brand of white or red wine in a box. At 22–28 pesos per liter, it isn't great wine but it's more drinkable than some of the more expensive bottled wines you'll encounter. However, "California" boxed wine is best if consumed within a few weeks of purchase, as it eventually develops an off taste from the packaging. L.A. Cetto is a good brand for more upscale Mexican wines. Most wine-loving cruisers that have been to the U.S. recently have a few bottles of Two Buck Chuck (Charles Shaw wine from Trader Joe's) tucked away in the bilges.

Other liquors: Most large grocery stores carry a few brands of vodka and whiskey, but not much gin *(ginebra)*. For particular brands, a large liquor store is a better bet.

ICE AND WATER:

Ice: *hielo* (pronounced like the color "yellow") Most stores and marinas have a freezer full of ice cubes for sale. These bags of ice are all from the *agua purificada* plant and should be safe.

Purified Water: *agua purificada* is available almost everywhere. It is sold in tiendas in bottles, gallon jugs, and 5–gallon jeroboams. Water companies also deliver to some marinas. Some communities even have automated *agua purificada* vending machines where you can refill your own containers for a few pesos. When ordering bottled water in a restaurant, the waiter may ask if you want *mineral* or *natural*. If you want still water, you can also ask for *agua sin gas*. Soda water is *agua con gas*. To get a glass of ordinary water someplace where you know *agua purificada* is used, ask for *agua de la llave* (tap water) or *agua de casa* (house water).

PET FOODS:

Both dry and canned dog food (*alimento para perros*) and cat food (*alimento para gatos*) are sold in most stores. The brands you will commonly see are Pedigree and Purina. Some vets carry Science Diet or other prescription brands. In small *tiendas*, you may find dry dog or cat food sold by the kilo in unlabeled plastic bags. The brand is probably Purina or Pedigree. Some *mercados* have a Purina store, selling all types of animal chows by the kilo from open 50–pound bags.

PAPER GOODS:

Facial Tissues: *pañuelos desechable* Kleenex brand is common.
  Paper Napkins: se*rvilletas desechable*
  Paper Plates: *platos de cartón*
  Paper Towels: *toallas de papel*
  Toilet Paper: *papel sanitario*

HEALTH AND BEAUTY PRODUCTS:

Conditioner: *acondicionador*
  Deodorant: *desodorante, antitranspirante* Secret, Dove, Soft 'n Dri, and Lady Speedstick are found in large stores.
  Insect Repellent: *repelente de insectos* A common brand is *Autan* which seems to be pretty effective. *Bye Bye* is a citronella-based brand, but unfortunately it doesn't seem to be very effective.
  Razor Blades: *hojas de afeitar*
  Shampoo: *shampoo* A wide variety of shampoos and conditioners are available, including familiar brands such as L'Oreal, Dove, Herbal Essence, Pantene, Pert, VO5, and Head & Shoulders.
  Soap: *jabón*
  Sunscreen: *bloquedor solar, protección solar* Familiar brands include Hawaiian Tropic, Banana Boat, and Nivea.
  Toothpaste: *crema dental* Familiar brands include Colgate, Crest, and Arm & Hammer.
  Sanitary napkins: *toallas femeninas*
  Tampons: *tampones*

OTHER NONFOOD ITEMS:

Aluminum Foil: *papel aluminio*
  Bleach: *blanqueador* or *cloro*
  Dish detergent: *detergente concentrado para platos*
  Fly swatter: *matamoscas*
  Garbage Bags: *bolsas para basura*

Laundry Powder: *lavatrastes polvo, detergente polvo* The most common Mexican brands may contain bleach.

Matches: *cerillos*

Plastic Wrap: Not commonly found, but you may occasionally see *película autoadherente.*

Straws: *popotes*

Waxed Paper: *papel encerado*

SPANISH COOKING TERMS

The following vocabulary items will help you interpret instructions on Mexican packaged foods or follow a local recipe.

Measurements:

cuchara: tablespoon
cucharita: teaspoon
jarra: jar
lata: can
libra: pound
media: half
onza: ounce
pizca: pinch
pieza: piece
taza: cup

Cooking Terms:

ablandar: tenderize
agregar: add
asar: grill
azotar: whip
barbacoa: pit-roasted
caldo: broth
cocer: cook
cocer a fuego bajo: simmer
cocidas: cooked
combinar: combine
congelado(a): frozen
cortar: cut
crudo(a): raw

cubrir: cover
derretir: melt
destrozar: shred
disolver: dissolve
en polva: powdered
escurrir (vacia de liquido): drain
estufa: stove
freír: fry
fresco(a): fresh
fuego: fire
horno: oven
horno de microondas: microwave oven
lento: slow
licuan: liquefy, blend
marinar: marinate
hervir: boil
mesclar: toss or mix
moler: grind
molido: ground
pelar: peel
picar: chop
puré: pureé
rallado: grated
rallar: grate
rebanar: slice
recipiente: receptacle
remover: stir
rostizada: roasted on a spit or grill
saltear: sauté
seco(a): dried
tapa: lid, cover
vapor: steam
vacier: empty

Sometimes it's better to do your own translation.

On some Mexican products you may see an English translation of the directions. Sometimes the translation is helpful; sometimes it isn't. Here's an exact transcript of directions I once found on a package of spaghetti: "Preparation Way: In 2 lt. of boiling water to drain the contents of this package with salt. Move constantly to avoid it's to adhere. The noodle and little pasta need to fry until to glid. After add 2 lt. of season water or animal broth or chiken broth." I presume the instructions were for noodle soup, but I'm not sure!

Things to bring from the U.S.

WHEN CONSIDERING WHAT ITEMS you might want to bring with you from the U.S. or Canada, remember that people eat everywhere and you will be able to buy food wherever you go. You could cook and eat comfortably anywhere in Mexico without bringing anything with you from the U.S. However, some items you are used to will not be available in Mexico. Only you can decide what foods and other products are important to your comfort. Take a look at the list below as well as the discussion in Ingredients and Cooking Terms and develop your own list of essentials to bring with you to Mexico. If you are bringing your boat down from Southern California, you may wish to wait until you reach Ensenada, Mexico before doing your major provisioning. Cruisers note that in Ensenada they are able to buy the same foods that are available in Southern California, but generally at lower prices. If you are already in Mexico and you have visitors coming south to meet you, you may ask them to bring supplies or specialty items.

> ### Visitors are wonderful!
>
> Having friends or family come visit you in Mexico is a great way to replenish hard-to-find supplies. When our friend, Mike, joined us in Barra de Navidad we asked him to bring several items including a case of the special dog food our dogs eat, our mail, and a few boat parts we ordered. I'm sure he thought he was bringing coals to Newcastle when I asked him to bring six cans of diced green chiles with him! However, mild green poblano chiles are commonly available fresh, but not canned, in Mexico.

Be careful not to load up too much on food. It's not the end of the world if you run out of something, so it's probably better to under buy than over buy. Remember that everything you buy will have to be stored somewhere on your boat. Spend some time in advance exploring the storage spaces on your boat and figuring out how much space is available and what should be stored where. Make sure to include your partner in this exploration so you don't discover that both of you have designs on the same storage locker! I've found it helpful to draw a map of the storage spaces in the boat with notes about what items are stored in each location. We have some deeply buried storage spaces on Legacy where it would be easy to lose things if we didn't keep an inventory!

PAPER PRODUCTS:

Older cruising guides frequently encouraged cruisers to bring large quantities of paper products with them to Mexico. Paper towels, toilet paper, paper napkins, and tissues are widely available in Mexico. Common brands may not be of the quality you prefer, but U.S. brand toilet paper and paper towels are available in most larger stores. For convenience, I bring a Costco case each of paper towels and toilet paper, as well as a large package of paper napkins. This requires a great deal of storage room on board, though. I store extra paper products in kayaking-style dry bags, which we stash in out-of-the-way storage spots on board.

PLASTIC BAGS:

While thin plastic bags are used extensively in Mexico, Ziploc bags are worth their weight in gold on a boat! I bring a couple of boxes each of every size from snack size to 2-gallon bags. I also like to use the Ziploc veggie bags that, unfortunately, are rarely available in the U.S. I've found that you can buy them if you are living or traveling in Canada, or direct by mail order from Johnson and Johnson. Because Ziploc bags are so valuable to me, I wash and reuse them until worn out. We frequently have Ziploc bags fastened to Legacy's lifelines with clothespins, drying in the sun. I also wash and reuse FoodSaver bags. We need to replace them after a few uses, however, so I carry several rolls of bag material on board.

In addition to regular Ziploc bags and FoodSaver bags, it is also useful to have a few "Packmate" style bags that allow you to press the air out of the bag to store or pack items. These are useful for storage of infrequently used clothes, extra linens, and other soft objects. My husband carries a microfiber TravelSmith blazer and slacks

> **Plastic bags are used for everything in Mexico:**
>
> We've been amazed by the different uses for thin plastic bags in Mexico. Mexicans use them not only in common ways such as to bag produce, meat, or fish, but in lots of innovative ways. When ordering take-out food (*para llevar*), we have received a selection of condiments all neatly bagged in plastic, including salsa, guacamole, pickled onions, grated cucumber, and chiles. At restaurants, we've seen kids served chocolate milk or other drinks in a plastic bag with the top knotted around a straw! We reuse plastic produce bags to clean up after our dogs or to contain small amounts of trash.

for unexpected dressy occasions and stores them in a Packmate bag. If we have to travel to a wedding or funeral, a quick tumble in a clothes drier restores them to a wearable state.

CANNED GOODS:

Your selection of canned goods will be very personal and will be based on your cooking needs. Look through your favorite recipes and compare them to the ingredients discussed in Ingredients and Cooking Terms. This will help you develop your own list of must-have items. I tend to stock up on diced tomatoes, tomato sauce, tomato paste, diced green chiles, sliced and diced black olives, chicken broth, kidney beans, soup (especially tomato), pickle relish, mandarin oranges, and crushed pineapple.

You might think that beans and tomato products would be readily available in Mexico, but that hasn't been my experience. Canned beans are available but are usually refried (*frijoles refritos*) or black beans (*frijoles negros entero*). Kidney beans (*frijoles bayo entero*) are much harder to find. Campbell's tomato soup is available, but the seasoning and texture is somewhat different from the U.S. product. Canned tomatoes frequently have seasoning added and are not always available diced. *Pure de Tomate* is sold in cans that look like tomato paste or tomato sauce, but it is actually a thin tomato puree with a bit of spice.

We also like to stock up on shelf-stable bacon, available in retort packaging at Costco and other stores. Although Mexican bacon is excellent, the precooked shelf-stable bacon is fast and involves minimal cleanup. We use it for breakfast, as well as for BLTs or, more commonly in Mexico, BTAs (bacon, tomato, and avocado sandwiches).

STAPLES:

I bring a couple of bags each of flour and sugar, but find that Mexican products make fine substitutes. Standard Mexican sugar, however, is often coarser than U.S. brands, and is sometimes light beige in color. I also bring cornmeal, oatmeal, a small can of shortening, baking powder, baking soda, and yeast. Although most of those products are available in Mexico, I like to bring familiar brands since one package will last all season. We use a lot of peanut butter, so I bring several Costco twin-packs of my favorite brand. Plain rice is readily available in Mexico, however, I bring a bag or two of specialty rices, such as Thai jasmine rice.

SPICES:

I'm pretty picky about my spices. The color and taste of spices deteriorate quickly in the heat, so each summer I buy new spices while back in the U.S. Red-colored spices and green herbs need to be replaced most frequently. Other spices, you can probably keep for two years. Spices can be expensive, so I buy in small quantities. Penzey's Spices (www.penzeys.com, mail order or retail outlets) have reasonable prices and sell most herbs and spices in ¼-cup plastic jars. I bring an ounce or two of bay leaves (which is a good-size bag) because I put bay leaves in my canisters of flour, Bisquick, cornmeal, and other staples to keep out bugs. The recipes you typically cook will govern the number and type of spices that you carry aboard. For the list of spices I keep aboard Legacy, see Appendix: What would you find in Legacy's galley?

BOXED SIDE DISHES:

Quick side dishes are uncommon in Mexico, except for basic items such as mashed potato flakes and a few pasta dishes. Because these are a nice addition to a simple chicken breast or piece of fish, I bring a variety of rice, pasta, couscous, and potato side dishes.

BAKING MIXES:

Except for pancake mix, these are fairly rare and expensive in Mexico so bring what you think you will need. For me, a plain baking mix such as Bisquick is a staple and I bring a couple of large boxes. In addition, muffin mixes, cookie and cake mixes, pudding mixes, brownie mixes, and similar items allow an occasional treat or make a quick dessert to carry along to a potluck dinner.

SPECIALTY ITEMS:

What is important to you? Many cruisers bring chocolate chips and nuts for baking. I bring walnuts and slivered almonds for baking, and cashews and pistachios for snacking. Although raisins are available in larger markets, I also like to have dried apricots and dates on hand as well.

Other special items might include jarred items such as pesto, martini olives, kalamata olive spread, or pickled vegetables. Trader Joe's carries a variety of interesting spreads that make good appetizers when smeared on crackers, tortillas, or crostini. Because of our Pacific Northwest roots, we also carry retort pouches of smoked wild Alaska salmon and cans of smoked salmon pate. Those are always a hit at dinghy raft-ups and other potlucks!

If you enjoy a particular type of soda other than Coke and Pepsi, you might want to bring some along with you. For us, that means Diet Dr. Pepper and Diet 7-Up, although the latter is often available in larger stores. Other cruisers have said that they can taste a difference in diet Coke and Pepsi between the U.S. and Mexico, but we've never been bothered by the difference.

HOLIDAY ITEMS:

Think about what foods are important to you at holidays and consider bringing along one or more of them. A can of pumpkin for a pie or can of cranberry sauce don't take up much room on board, but can bring a lot of pleasure if you are cruising at Thanksgiving for the first time. These items are sometimes available at Wal-Mart and other large stores in Mexico, but generally sell out well before Thanksgiving. Do you have to have your grandmother's green bean casserole? Bring along cans of green beans and French fried onions, or whatever else you need. On Legacy, we also carry a small (loaf pan size) plastic container with Christmas stockings and a few decorations. We find that we don't exchange large or expensive presents while cruising, but have a wonderful time finding local candies and other small items to fill each other's stocking.

Even though you bring along a few holiday items, be flexible. You may want to establish new traditions using locally available items or use traditional items in a non-traditional way. We attended one Thanksgiving dinner where the chefs made a wonderful diced apple and dried cranberry compote because they were unable to find other types of cranberries. It was a delicious substitute for cranberry sauce.

MEAT—YES OR NO:

This is a touchy question, since customs and agricultural rules change frequently. It may also depend on where you plan to enter Mexico. Many cruisers have had meat products seized at Cabo San Lucas. In 2003, agricultural inspectors seized all California poultry from incoming boats. The next year, many cruisers had all of their U.S. meat and poultry impounded at Cabo. In recent years, bringing beef across international borders has been difficult. Arriving in Mexico by car, we've never had an inspector ask us about meat. If you are planning to bring meat with you, carefully consider how badly you want particular types of meat and how much you are willing to risk to impoundment.

Our first year in Mexico, we were disappointed by the meats (especially beef) that we were able to buy in the supermarkets. In subsequent years, though, we've learned to find good meats in specialty markets and through sources that cater to gringos. We've had good luck buying meat in San Carlos, Mazatlan, Puerto Vallarta, and through Maria in Barra de Navidad. When in doubt, ask other cruisers for recommendations.

Substitutions, Conversions, and Rules of Thumb

W HEN COOKING AND FOOD SHOPPING IN MEXICO, the most important rule is to be flexible. By using the tips in this book and experimenting a little bit, you'll soon learn to successfully adapt your favorite recipes to use available ingredients.

HOW TO ADAPT *GRINGO* RECIPES:

Don't discount a recipe just because you don't have all of the ingredients called for. When adapting a recipe, I read through the ingredients and identify those that may be problematic. Then considering each ingredient, decide if the ingredient is essential and, if so, what could substitute for it. Missing a spice? Think about what other flavors might complement the dish. Don't have a particular fresh vegetable? Try canned or substitute a different vegetable altogether. For example, jicama makes a good substitute for water chestnuts.

Experiment with different cheeses in your favorite recipes. If you pay attention to whether a cheese is melting or non-melting, you may end up with a great variation on a favorite recipe. Below you will find some specific suggestions on substituting ingredients in your recipes.

SUBSTITUTIONS:

The list below is merely a starting point. Don't be afraid to branch out. It's really rare for an altered recipe to be inedible and, on those rare occasions, you probably have a can of soup handy or eggs that you can scramble for dinner!

Baking Powder (1 teaspoon):

Substitute ¼ teaspoon baking soda and ½ cup yogurt; or ½ teaspoon baking soda and ½ teaspoon cream of tartar.

Butter (1 cup):

Substitute ¾ cup vegetable oil.

Buttermilk (1 cup):

Substitute 1 cup yogurt or *crema*; or add 2 tablespoons vinegar or lemon (or lime) juice to 1 cup warm milk, let stand 10 minutes.

Cake Flour (1 cup):

Substitute 1 cup minus 2 tablespoons all-purpose flour.

Cheese Substitutions:

For Cheddar, substitute *Asadero, Chihuahua* or *Manchego*.
For Mozzarella, substitute *Oaxaco* or *Panela*.
For Muenster, substitute *Chihuahua*.
For Parmesan, substitute *Anejo*.
For Provolone, substitute *Asadero*.
For Ricotta, substitute *Panela, Queso Fresco,* or *Requeson*.

Chocolate, Unsweetened (1 ounce):

Substitute 3 tablespoons cocoa and 1 tablespoon butter.

Coconut Milk (1 cup):

Simmer 1 cup milk and ½ cup dried coconut (not sweetened) for 20 minutes, cool and strain.

Cornstarch (for thickening, 1 tablespoon):

Substitute 2 tablespoons flour or 4 teaspoons quick-cooking tapioca.

Egg (1):

Substitute 2 tablespoons cooking oil in baked goods, however item won't be as light.

Herbs:

Substitute 1 teaspoon dried herbs for 1 tablespoon fresh herbs.

Ketchup or chili sauce (for use in cooking, 1 cup):

Substitute 1 cup tomato sauce, ½ cup sugar, and 2 tablespoons vinegar.

Lemon Juice (1 tablespoon):

Substitute 1 tablespoon lime juice or ½ tablespoon vinegar. Use the vinegar substitution when lemon juice is used for its acidity, not for flavor.

Milk (for baking, 1 cup):

Substitute 1 cup water and 1½ teaspoon butter.

Sesame Oil:

Sesame seeds are readily available in Mexico, however it is sometimes difficult to find sesame oil. To make your own, toast sesame seeds in a small skillet until golden brown. Remove from heat, add canola or other mild vegetable oil to the skillet and let stand for 30 minutes. If you wish, you can crush the sesame seeds to increase the flavor. Drain off oil and keep in a tightly sealed jar.

Sour Cream (1 cup):

Substitute 1 cup *crema* or substitute ⅓ cup butter plus ¾ cup yogurt.

Sugar, Brown (1 packed cup):

Substitute 1 cup white sugar, or 1 cup *piloncillo* (grated, then lightly packed into measuring cup).

Sugar, Granulated (1 cup):

Substitute ¾ cup honey or maple syrup, reduce liquids by ¼ cup.

Tomato Juice (1 cup):

Substitute ½ cup tomato sauce and ½ cup water.

Tomato Sauce (2 cups):

Substitute ¾ cup tomato paste and 1 cup water.

Tomato Soup (1 Can):

Substitute 1 cup tomato sauce and ¼ cup water.

Table 1: Internal Temperatures For Properly Cooked Meat and Fish

Fish	135°
Fish (rare, such as tuna)	125°
Chicken and Turkey	
White Meat	160–165°
Dark Meat	170–175 °
Beef and Lamb	
Rare	120–130°
Medium Rare	130–135°
Medium	140–150°
Medium Well	155–165°
Well Done	170–185°
Veal	
Medium	145–155°
Pork	
Pork Tenderloin	140–150°
Other cuts, medium	155–165°
Other cuts, well done	180–185°

The table below shows the amount of household chlorine bleach (4–6% sodium hypochlorite) to use when treating water in your vessel's tanks. If your tanks are partially full of treated water before adding water, reduce the amount of chlorine appropriately.

Table 2: Proper Amounts of Chlorine for Dosing Water Tanks

Size of Water Tank in Gallons	Amount of Chlorine Needed
10	1 tsp.
15	1 ½ tsp.
20	2 tsp.
25	2 ½ tsp.
30	1 tbsp.
40	4 tsp.
50	5 tsp.
60	2 tbsp.
70	2 tbsp. plus 1 tsp.
80	2 tbsp. plus 2 tsp.
90	3 tbsp.
100	3 tbsp. plus 1 tsp.
110	3 tbsp. plus 2 tsp.
120	4 tbsp. or ¼ cup
130	4 tbsp. plus 1 tsp.
140	4 tbsp. plus 2 tsp.
150	5 tbsp.
160	5 tbsp. plus 1 tsp. or ⅓ cup
170	5 tbsp. plus 2 tsp.
180	6 tbsp.
190	6 tbsp. plus 1 tsp.
200	6 tbsp. plus 2 tsp.

In the table below, first find the cost in pesos per liter in the left column. Then follow across that line to the right to the current exchange rate in pesos per U.S. dollar. The result is the cost per gallon in U.S. dollars.

For example, if you pay 5 pesos per liter for diesel and the current exchange rate is 11 pesos per U.S. dollar, then the cost of the diesel is $1.76/gallon.

Table 3: Converting pesos/liter to US dollars/gallon

Cost in Pesos/Liter	Exchange Rate: Pesos/US Dollar						
	9	10	10.5	11	11.5	12	13
1	$0.43	$0.39	$0.37	$0.35	$0.34	$0.32	$0.30
2	$0.86	$0.78	$0.74	$0.70	$0.67	$0.65	$0.60
3	$1.29	$1.16	$1.11	$1.06	$1.01	$0.97	$0.89
4	$1.72	$1.55	$1.48	$1.41	$1.35	$1.29	$1.19
4.5	$1.94	$1.74	$1.66	$1.59	$1.52	$1.45	$1.34
5	$2.15	$1.94	$1.85	$1.76	$1.68	$1.61	$1.49
5.5	$2.37	$2.13	$2.03	$1.94	$1.85	$1.78	$1.64
6	$2.58	$2.33	$2.21	$2.11	$2.02	$1.94	$1.79
6.5	$2.80	$2.52	$2.40	$2.29	$2.19	$2.10	$1.94
7	$3.01	$2.71	$2.58	$2.47	$2.36	$2.26	$2.09
7.5	$3.23	$2.91	$2.77	$2.64	$2.53	$2.42	$2.24
8	$3.44	$3.10	$2.95	$2.82	$2.70	$2.58	$2.38
8.5	$3.66	$3.29	$3.14	$2.99	$2.86	$2.74	$2.53
9	$3.88	$3.49	$3.32	$3.17	$3.03	$2.91	$2.68
10	$4.31	$3.88	$3.69	$3.52	$3.37	$3.23	$2.98
11	$4.74	$4.26	$4.06	$3.88	$3.71	$3.55	$3.28
12	$5.17	$4.65	$4.43	$4.23	$4.04	$3.88	$3.58
13	$5.60	$5.04	$4.80	$4.58	$4.38	$4.20	$3.88
14	$6.03	$5.43	$5.17	$4.93	$4.72	$4.52	$4.17
15	$6.46	$5.81	$5.54	$5.28	$5.05	$4.84	$4.47
16	$6.89	$6.20	$5.90	$5.64	$5.39	$5.17	$4.77
17	$7.32	$6.59	$6.27	$5.99	$5.73	$5.49	$5.07
18	$7.75	$6.98	$6.64	$6.34	$6.07	$5.81	$5.37
19	$8.18	$7.36	$7.01	$6.69	$6.40	$6.14	$5.66
20	$8.61	$7.75	$7.38	$7.05	$6.74	$6.46	$5.96

In the table below, first find the number of liters purchased in the left column. Then follow the line across to the right until you find the approximate number of pesos paid. Follow that column back up to the top to find the price per gallon in U.S. dollars. This table assumes an exchange rate of 10 pesos per U.S. dollar. If the exchange rate is less than 10 pesos/dollar, then the price per gallon will be higher. If the exchange rate is more than 10 pesos/dollar, then the price per gallon will be lower.

For example, if you buy 100 liters of diesel for about 700 pesos, then the price per gallon will be about $2.75.

Table 4: Converting Liters Purchased in Pesos to US Dollars/gallon
Exchange rate: 10 pesos/US Dollar

Number of liters purchased	Price per gallon in US Dollars												
	$1.00	$1.25	$1.50	$1.75	$2.00	$2.25	$2.50	$2.75	$3.00	$3.25	$3.50	$3.75	$4.00
1	2.6	3.2	3.9	4.5	5.2	5.8	6.5	7.1	7.7	8.4	9.0	9.7	10.3
10	26	32	39	45	52	58	65	71	77	84	90	97	103
20	52	65	77	90	103	116	129	142	155	168	181	194	206
30	77	97	116	135	155	174	194	213	232	252	271	290	310
40	103	129	155	181	206	232	258	284	310	335	361	387	413
50	129	161	194	226	258	290	323	355	387	419	452	484	516
60	155	194	232	271	310	348	387	426	465	503	542	581	619
70	181	226	271	316	361	406	452	497	542	587	632	677	723
80	206	258	310	361	413	465	516	568	619	671	723	774	826
90	232	290	348	406	465	523	581	639	697	755	813	871	929
100	258	323	387	452	516	581	645	710	774	839	903	968	1,032
120	310	387	465	542	619	697	774	852	929	1,006	1,084	1,161	1,239
140	361	452	542	632	723	813	903	994	1,084	1,174	1,265	1,355	1,445
150	387	484	581	677	774	871	968	1,065	1,161	1,258	1,355	1,452	1,548
200	516	645	774	903	1,032	1,161	1,290	1,419	1,548	1,677	1,806	1,935	2,065
250	645	806	968	1,129	1,290	1,452	1,613	1,774	1,935	2,097	2,258	2,419	2,581
300	774	968	1,161	1,355	1,548	1,742	1,935	2,129	2,323	2,516	2,710	2,903	3,097
400	1,032	1,290	1,548	1,806	2,065	2,323	2,581	2,839	3,097	3,355	3,613	3,871	4,129
500	1,290	1,613	1,935	2,258	2,581	2,903	3,226	3,548	3,871	4,194	4,516	4,839	5,161

If you are quoted a price in U.S. dollars per liter, you can use the table below to convert the price to U.S. dollars per gallon. Simply find the price/liter in the left column and read across to find the price/gallon in the right column.

For example, if you are quoted a price for diesel of $.60/liter, then you are paying $2.33/gallon for the fuel.

Table 5: Converting US Dollars/liter to US Dollars/gallon

US DOLLARS/LITER	US DOLLARS/GALLON
$0.10	$0.39
$0.20	$0.78
$0.30	$1.16
$0.40	$1.55
$0.50	$1.94
$0.60	$2.33
$0.70	$2.71
$0.80	$3.10
$0.90	$3.49
$1.00	$3.88
$1.10	$4.26
$1.20	$4.65
$1.30	$5.04
$1.40	$5.43
$1.50	$5.81
$1.60	$6.20
$1.70	$6.59
$1.80	$6.98
$1.90	$7.36
$2.00	$7.75

In the table below, first find the price per kilogram in the left column. Then follow the line across to the right until you reach the column for the current exchange rate in pesos per U.S. dollar. The result is the price in U.S. dollars per pound.

For example, if you buy shrimp for 110 pesos per kilogram, and the current exchange rate is 10 pesos per U.S. dollar, then the cost of the shrimp is $5.01 per pound.

Table 6: Converting pesos/kilogram to US dollars/pound

COST IN PESOS/KILOGRAM	EXCHANGE RATE: PESOS/US DOLLAR				
	9	10	11	12	13
1	$0.05	$0.05	$0.04	$0.04	$0.04
2	$0.10	$0.09	$0.08	$0.08	$0.07
3	$0.15	$0.14	$0.12	$0.11	$0.11
4	$0.20	$0.18	$0.17	$0.15	$0.14
5	$0.25	$0.23	$0.21	$0.19	$0.18
6	$0.30	$0.27	$0.25	$0.23	$0.21
7	$0.35	$0.32	$0.29	$0.27	$0.25
8	$0.40	$0.36	$0.33	$0.30	$0.28
9	$0.46	$0.41	$0.37	$0.34	$0.32
10	$0.51	$0.46	$0.41	$0.38	$0.35
15	$0.76	$0.68	$0.62	$0.57	$0.53
20	$1.01	$0.91	$0.83	$0.76	$0.70
25	$1.26	$1.14	$1.03	$0.95	$0.88
30	$1.52	$1.37	$1.24	$1.14	$1.05
35	$1.77	$1.59	$1.45	$1.33	$1.23
40	$2.02	$1.82	$1.65	$1.52	$1.40
45	$2.28	$2.05	$1.86	$1.71	$1.58
50	$2.53	$2.28	$2.07	$1.90	$1.75
60	$3.03	$2.73	$2.48	$2.28	$2.10
70	$3.54	$3.19	$2.90	$2.65	$2.45
80	$4.04	$3.64	$3.31	$3.03	$2.80
90	$4.55	$4.10	$3.72	$3.41	$3.15
100	$5.06	$4.55	$4.14	$3.79	$3.50
110	$5.56	$5.01	$4.55	$4.17	$3.85
120	$6.07	$5.46	$4.96	$4.55	$4.20
130	$6.57	$5.92	$5.38	$4.93	$4.55
140	$7.08	$6.37	$5.79	$5.31	$4.90
150	$7.58	$6.83	$6.20	$5.69	$5.25
200	$10.11	$9.10	$8.27	$7.58	$7.00

Local Provisioning Information

CABO SAN LUCAS:

The local hailing channel is VHF-22, and the local net is 8 a.m. daily. Cabo San Lucas is expensive and full of tourists, so most cruisers don't spend much time here. However, many cruisers stop at Cabo briefly to check in and reprovision after coming down the outside of the Baja Peninsula from California. Cabo has the full range of large grocery stores and "big box" stores such as Costco and City Club. In addition, downtown there are a couple of medium-size *tiendas* and many convenience stores near the marina and anchorage areas. Aramburo's Market, about a block north of the harbormaster's office, is a cruiser favorite for provisioning without resorting to a bus or cab ride.

About two blocks inland from the west end of the Marina Cabo San Lucas, we found a very nice gourmet store selling good wines, cheeses, smoked salmon, and other luxury items. Swiss Pastry, at the corner of Hidalgo and Lázaro Cárdenas has excellent bagels and other pastries. Tortillería Perla, at the corner of Calle Abasolo and Calle 16 de Septiembre, is a convenient place to buy both corn and flour tortillas.

LA PAZ:

Local hailing channel is VHF-22 and the local net is 8 a.m. Monday through Saturday. La Paz is a convenient place to provision. The downtown area is compact, and taxis are inexpensive and easy to find. For example, one or more taxis hang out in the parking lot of Marina de La Paz, as well as just outside the gates. Small buses, called *collectivos*, travel frequently along the major routes. The fare is five pesos, and their routes are written on the windshield of the van-style school buses. Marina de La Paz, Marina Don Jose, Abaroa boatyard, and the main anchorage are all within walking distance of downtown. Marinas Palmira and Costa Baja are further out of town but offer regular shuttles to the downtown area.

Baja California is considered the Mexican "frontier" and has special exemptions from duties and regulations. As a result, you will find many more U.S. products in the stores at much more reasonable prices than on the mainland. For example, you can find Swiss Dairy brand half-and-half, whipping cream, and buttermilk in the dairy case of major stores.

The favorite large grocery store among cruisers is C.C.C. (pronounced "say-say-say") Colima. To get to C.C.C. Colima from the downtown marinas and dinghy docks, walk one block inland to Abasolo, which is a major road. Stand on the water side of Abasolo and catch any *collectivo* headed out of downtown. C.C.C. will be on the left side of Abasolo at Colima, and you will recognize it by the large parking lot with metal awnings providing shade, and by the Bancomer bank in the corner of the parking lot. After your shopping, you can return by *collectivo* or catch a cab for about 40 pesos. The C.C.C. is a well-supplied, full-service grocery store with good produce; excellent Sonoran beef in the freezer case; refrigerated specialty breads including pita, English muffins, and rye bread; Challenge and Tillamook butter; Jif and Skippy peanut butter; Bisquick and other baking mixes; marshmallow crème; good oils and vinegars; Asian products; and many U.S. Springfield-brand products.

In the downtown area, there is a medium-size Ley (affiliated with Safeway) on 5 de Mayo, and two Aramburo's groceries which are very good. The larger Aramburo's store is at the corner of Madero and Hidalgo — look for the cow hanging from the front of the building. Aramburo's carries many Springfield-brand products as well as a nice selection of specialty oils and vinegars, Hershey's unsweetened baking chocolate, Betty Crocker pie crust mix, cake mixes and canned frosting.

Along the highway leading to Cabo San Lucas, about a 50-peso taxi ride from the downtown marinas, you will find Soriana and City Club. Soriana is a large full-service grocery store, but carries fewer U.S. products than C.C.C. City Club is a membership warehouse than seems to be like a small Sam's Club. One-day membership passes may be purchased for 20 pesos. You pick up the pass from the membership desk on your way in, but pay for it along with your purchases at the cashier. City Club is a good place to buy case lots of soda and beer. They even have 12-packs of soda, including A&W diet root beer at a fraction of the price I paid in Puerto Vallarta. Other interesting products include Peter Pan peanut butter, six packs of assorted picante sauces, Dial anti-bacterial liquid hand soap, and large jars containing 100 single-use "bubbles" of shampoo.

La Paz also has two small central *mercados*. Cruisers noted that the "Bravo Market" at Bravo and Prieto has a couple of excellent *carnecerías* and very good fish counters. The "Municipal Market" at Degollado and Revolucion is slightly larger and has clothing and other stalls in addition to meat, fish, and produce. Surrounding the markets are several *tortillerías* and cruisers especially recommend Tortillería Gladys on Revolucion. Flour tortillas are particularly good on the Baja Peninsula. The *mercados* are within walking distance of the downtown marinas, or stand on the inland side of Abasolo and catch any *collectivo* heading downtown, if you wish to ride.

In addition to the major markets, there are some special finds in La Paz. Near the Bravo Market, on Ramirez between Bravo and Rosales, you will find Café La Virtud. In addition to regular baked goods, Virtud offers low-calorie items and carbohydrate-balanced baked goods for diabetics. They also sell interesting jams made with fructose.

Along the *malecon* in downtown La Paz you will find one of our favorite ice cream stops, La Fuente, across from the municipal pier. Look for the polka-dot tree. La Fuente carries some of the most interesting ice cream flavors we've seen, including guava, tequila-almond, Kahlua, and *elote* (corn).

La Paz is also a good place to get *arrachera* (flank steak). Three blocks up Legaspi from the downtown marinas, you will find Las Arracheras, which sells excellent *arrachera*, either marinated or unmarinated, as well as good frozen steaks and other meats. If you are too hungry to make it back to your boat with your purchases, you will find cruiser-favorite Rancho Viejo restaurant about one block up Legaspi from the marinas. Rancho Viejo offers excellent *arrachera* and other barbecued meats to eat in or take out (*para llevar*). We like to get one kilo of *arrachera* takeout, which makes one large dinner and two lunches for us at a cost of about 170 pesos. The *arrachera* comes with grilled onion, hot tortillas, three kinds of salsa, and a condiment tray containing pickled onions, sliced cucumbers, lime wedges, grated cabbage, and roasted chiles.

Another good source of takeout food is Imelda, who sets up a stand outside the gate of Marina de La Paz most mornings. She sells wonderful tamales, burritos, empanadas, chiles relleno, and enchiladas at very reasonable prices.

AGUA VERDE:

The local hailing channel is VHF-16, and there is no local net. Agua Verde is a small, quite remote village on the Baja Peninsula. I've included it even though Agua Verde isn't a normal reprovisioning stop. The *tienda* at Agua Verde is surprisingly well-stocked for such a remote village. However, there isn't any electricity in Agua Verde, except for a few houses with solar panels, so use caution if purchasing any items that need refrigeration.

The *tienda* is found on the northwest side of the wash that runs through the village. If you can't find it readily, one of the local kids would be happy to serve as your guide. Once at the *tienda*, it may be hard to tell what is available. There will be crates of fruits and vegetables, a number of coolers, and a side room with shelves containing a few canned goods and sundries. The proprietress will likely suggest items that you may need. The village is well-known for the locally-made goat cheese; ask the proprietress if any is available. If the *tienda* has recently been re-supplied, the coolers will contain ice as well as perishable items. We were able to buy icy cold fresh milk from one of the coolers when a shipment of supplies had just come in.

> ### Don't get roasted goat for Thanksgiving!
>
> Cruisers sometimes order roasted young goat for Easter in Agua Verde. One group thought that was a great idea, and ordered a roasted goat for Thanksgiving dinner. The results weren't what they expected, since they failed to realize that by November those cute little baby goats are adults and no longer tender and sweet.

If you need tortillas, let the store owner know and she will send one of her children off to the local tortilla maker to collect them while you shop. Many times, the tortillas will be warm and freshly made while you wait. There is a large herd of goats in the community and some cruisers have arranged to purchase a roasted young goat during the springtime months.

LORETO AND PUERTO ESCONDIDO:

Local hailing channel is VHF-16 and the local net is at 8 a.m. daily on VHF-22. Loreto is a very nice little town with several good shops, but unfortunately it's not the most convenient place to provision. The anchorage at Puerto Escondido is about 13 miles from the town of Loreto and transportation is difficult. In calm conditions, it is possible to anchor off Loreto long enough to provision but it isn't a safe overnight anchorage.

You have several options for getting to town from Puerto Escondido. The first is to ask on the morning net if anyone can give you a ride or if there are other people who

Baby goats are common in Agua Verde in the spring. Some cruisers will order roasted goat for a special dinner. (Joan Stockard photo)

would like to share a taxi. Taxis are generally waiting by the dinghy dock during the morning hours; be sure to negotiate the price before getting into the cab. Taxi prices are high, about 350 pesos for a one-way trip and 600 pesos for a round trip. Rental cars are available for U.S. $40 to $80 per day (not including tax and insurance) and all of the companies will deliver cars to the dinghy dock. It is also possible to catch a bus into town if you walk about ¾ of a mile out to Highway 1, however it's important to determine the bus schedule because there are only a few each day.

Within walking distance of the anchorage, there are two small *tiendas*. About ¼ mile from the dinghy dock is Tripui RV Park, which includes a restaurant and a small *tienda* selling a small selection of items. About ¾ mile, at the intersection with Highway 1, is Willy's *tienda*, which has a slightly better selection. Both *tienda*s carry a few fresh items, tortillas, canned goods, liquor, and ice.

In Loreto, the two largest supermarkets are El Pescador at the corner of Salvatierra and Independencia, and the ISSSTE store just north of the town plaza. The ISSSTE store carries mainly nonperishable items, while El Pescador is a full grocery store with produce, meat, and dairy products.

There are several smaller places that may be of interest to cruisers. There is a good *fruitería* on Juarez, just west of the intersection with Madero. Also on Madero at the intersection of Carrillo is Super Pan Garcia, which sells bread, *pan dulce*, and cakes.

Two blocks west on Misioneros between Carrillo and Constituyentes are three places of interest: Esperanza, the "Pork Lady"; a large Pacifico *deposito*; and El Sarape; all on the right hand side when headed north. The "Pork Lady" butchers a hog each Monday and is sometimes out of pork by Saturday. She will cut to order whatever piece of pig you want. El Sarape is a small *tienda* that carries bulk dry goods, bulk cat and dog food, baking supplies, heavyweight plastic bags by the pound, and other items. One of the women working in the store speaks English well.

On Ayuntamienta north of Heroes de la Independencia, you will find another good small *tienda*, called Mercadito Davis Rubio. This *tienda* carries decent produce, good smoked pork chops, packaged chicken, excellent bulk bacon, and a variety of other items. As with other small *tienda*s in Mexico, if you don't see what you need, ask. They have additional coolers in the back room.

Two other finds are near the main street into town (Paseo Pedro de Ugarte) just a few blocks from Highway 1. On Highway 1, just south of the turn into Loreto is a brick convenience store. If you turn immediately before the convenience store, you will find Mini-Super La Gigante. In addition to the small selection of groceries he carries, the owner, Sergio, will cut and grind beef, and sometimes pork, to order. His hamburger is famous among cruisers. I ordered a kilo of *carne molida para hamburgesas* and watched him pull beef from the freezer, slice it and trim it of fat, and grind it twice. When he plopped the plastic bag of ground beef on the scale, it was exactly one kilo. When I commented on his obvious skill, he shrugged and said that he'd been grinding beef for 50 years. The other find, Bartollio's, is on Ugarte, the main street, and is a popular market with Mexicans. Bartollio's has an extensive meat department and will cut meat to order upon request.

Cruisers in Loreto and Escondido also speak highly of the Saturday market. It is just north of Loreto. When leaving Loreto, turn left near the *topes* (speed bumps) where the divided highway becomes two-way. It operates on Saturdays from about 8 a.m. until 2 or 3 and includes a number of stalls with nice fresh produce, meats, and other goods.

SANTA ROSALIA:

The local hailing channel is VHF-16 and there is no local net. While Santa Rosalia is small, reprovisioning for basic goods is easy. From the marina and anchorage in Santa Rosalia, there are several *tienda*s of interest within walking distance. If you want to go further afield, taxis are reasonable and readily available along the main street, Obregon. Most of the *tienda*s mentioned below are on either Obregon (the "up" street) or Constitución (the "down" street). Many cruisers check each *tienda* for available goods and figure that between all of them they will be able to get most of the items on their list.

A good place to start is near the Eiffel church. On the opposite corner is Mercadito San Jose, which carries canned goods, bread, tortillas, refrigerated items, eggs, and some produce. Also within view of the church is Tortilleria Santa Agueda. This is a fun place to watch workers make wonderful thin Baja flour tortillas by hand while you wait for your purchase to be packaged. One worker uses a press to turn lumps of dough into flat discs, then tosses them onto the grill. A second worker flips the tortillas back and forth until they're cooked. Another takes the cooked tortillas and tosses them onto cooling grates. Once you order a kilo or half kilo (*media kilo*) of tortillas, the cashier counts out the tortillas, bags them, and takes your money.

Continuing up Obregon, you will find another landmark, Panadería El Boleo. This bakery reflects the French heritage of the community with baguettes, here called *pan birote*. Next door to the *panadería* is the ISSSTE *tienda*, which sells canned goods and other basic items to the public.

For good produce, continue up Obregon until you reach the Banamex bank. Turn right, walk one block, and turn right again, where you will find Fruitería La Sermana. The *fruitería* receives stock twice a week, Monday and Thursday on our last visit, and the best items sell out quickly. The friendly and attractive proprietress is a good person with whom to practice your Spanish. Unlike many other Mexicans, with *gringos* she speaks Spanish slowly and distinctly and listens carefully to understand their halting replies.

Other *tienda*s include Go4Value, which carries housewares and canned goods, Carnicería Delia, which carries meats, some produce, milk, and canned goods, and Mercado Nunez Brooks.

Any discussion of Santa Rosalia would be incomplete without a mention of Hot Dogs Chuyita, the famous hot dog vendor. Chuyita's stand opens each evening about 6 p.m. on the block between the Eiffel church and the town square. These delicious hot dogs are wrapped in bacon, fried, and topped with a variety of condiments and sauces. A couple of these hot dogs with everything (*con todo*) make a delicious and easy, but fat-laden, dinner.

Panadería El Boleo serves baked goods that reflect both the French and Mexican roots of Santa Rosalia. Unlike most *panaderías*, at El Boleo customers request items from behind the counter rather than helping themselves from the displays.

SAN CARLOS:

The local hailing channel is VHF-16 and the local net is on VHF-72 at 8 a.m. daily. Marina San Carlos is within walking distance of several *tiendas*. Marina Real is further out of town, but the marina office sometimes operates a shuttle to downtown San Carlos. Many cruisers keep cars in San Carlos, so you may also be able to catch rides to do your provisioning. Cruisers also take advantage of the bus that operates between San Carlos and Guaymas.

Within San Carlos, however, there are a number of options for food purchases. A short distance uphill from Marina San Carlos is Fruitería Bahía San Carlos, which carries produce, canned goods, meat, and refrigerated items. A short walk from the marina office is a *deposito* for beer, as well as Supermercado San Carlos for basic items. On the main street through San Carlos are several small *tiendas*. Of special note is Super Carnes Santa Rosa, across from Rosa's Cantina. This is a good place to get meat, as well as produce and other items. Super Izzy's is also a good option for canned goods, refrigerated items, and some meats.

A notable feature of San Carlos is the variety of veggie trucks operating in the area. Trucks visit the marinas and RV parks carrying nice produce, as well as shrimp, salsa, tortillas, burritos, and other prepared items. Alejandro visits both marinas with his bright red truck and sweet-talks customers into buying more items than they think they need. Behind Rosa's Cantina, you will find Tony's, a "veggie truck on steroids" that sets up from 11 a.m. until late afternoon every day except Sunday. Tony sets up on a lot shaded with metal awnings, and in addition to the produce truck, puts out a variety of coolers containing meat, sausage, fresh-squeezed fruit juices, prepared foods, cheese, dairy products, and other items. Tony also has some interesting breads at times.

For major provisioning, cruisers frequently drive to the Ley store on the main route into Guaymas, about 12 miles from San Carlos. This large full-service grocery store can meet most of your provisioning needs. Cruisers with cars will sometimes make the 2-hour drive to Hermosillo to visit Sam's Club, Home Depot, and Costco.

MAZATLAN:

The local hailing channel is VHF-22 and the local net is at 8 a.m., Monday through Saturday. Mazatlan is a great place to provision. It has a large variety of stores, and

At Tony's "veggie truck on steroids" in San Carlos, customers choose from a broad range of fruits and vegetables, as well as cheeses, breads, meat and seafood, juices, and prepared foods.

is easy to get around thanks to an excellent bus system. In the local cruisers' guide (available from the marina offices), you can find the bus routes that cruisers use most frequently. In addition to the buses, which run every 10 minutes or so, there are regular taxis; "pulmonias" (open golf-cart style taxis on a VW chassis); and small pickups with bench seating in the bed of the truck, known as "spiders". Regular taxis, such as EcoTaxi, tend to be cheaper than "pulmonias", while "spiders" are an economical option for a group of people.

Several large grocery stores are a convenient bus or taxi ride from the marinas, including Walmart, Sam's Club, Commercial, Gigante, Soriana and Ley. Mega-Commercial at Gran Plaza and Gigante are the easiest to reach by bus. Bus fare is 5–10 pesos, and a taxi back from these stores is about 60 pesos. Recently there have been rumors that a large shopping center with a Ley or Soriana will be built directly across from Marina Mazatlan, which would be a great convenience for cruisers.

Currently, there are only limited supplies within walking distance of the marinas. In the Tourist Zone near El Cid Marina, there are several small convenience stores. In 2005 a small Supermercado opened at Marina Mazatlan that carries beer, liquor, ice cream, canned goods, and sundries. A veggie truck and a seafood truck make stops

"Spiders" are an economical means of transport for groups of people in Mazatlan. Taxis, *pulmonias*, and spiders in Mazatlan will generally beep their horns at *gringos* standing by the side of the road to see if they want a ride. Check the price; if you are with a group, the fare may be cheaper than waiting for the bus.

at Marina Mazatlan three mornings a week. The water truck brings *agua purificado* to the marina docks three days a week.

Mazatlan also has a large central *mercado* in the downtown area. Here you will find meat and fish stalls, produce stands, small grocery sections, and a variety of clothes, shoes, and other nonfood items. Keep a close eye on your belongings, and don't carry a purse. When the *mercado* is crowded, especially during Carnival and other activities, pickpockets work the area. My shopping bag was slashed in the *mercado* during a busy Carnival weekend. Luckily, my wallet was not in the shopping bag.

A special find in Mazatlan is Henderson Prime Meat Cutters. Henderson's is a small *carnecería* with very good meat, including Angus beef. All of the meat is kept frozen, cut to order, and vacuum-sealed in plastic. Henderson has very reasonable prices on beef, pork, and boneless chicken breasts. They will custom grind and package meat for hamburger and, if you wish, freeze it for later pickup. Lamb is sold during the spring, and around Thanksgiving and Christmas whole frozen turkeys are available. To get to Henderson Meats by bus, take the Sabalo Cocos bus past Gigante and Office Depot. The bus will make a left turn and then a right turn at Rincon de las Plazas. A couple of blocks after the right turn, watch for "Lavanderia Alejandro", a blue building on the left. Henderson Meats is next to the Lavanderia.

Mazatlan is also a good place to resupply the liquor cabinet. Most grocery stores carry beer, wine, rum, and tequila. For a selection of good wines and less common liquors, try Casa Arias on the Malecon. Take the Sabalo Centro bus to the stop for the aquarium (look for the sea lion statue on the right or ask the driver for the *aquario*). Casa Arias carries a large selection of fine wines, including French, Italian, Chilean, Spanish, Mexican, and California wines. In addition to a wide selection of tequila, rum, and brandy, they also carry a good selection of familiar brands of gin (Beefeaters, Tangueray, and Bombay Sapphire), whiskey (Glenlivit, Chivas Regal, and Jack Daniels), vodka (Grey Goose, Stoli, Finlandia, and Absolut), and liqueurs (Frangelico, Bailey's, and Kahlua). Casa Arias also carries a small selection of gourmet foods including meats, cheeses, canned goods, oils, vinegars, and mixers.

PUERTO VALLARTA AND BANDERAS BAY:

Local hailing channel is VHF-22 and the local net is at 8:30 a.m., Monday through Saturday. Within Banderas Bay, there are popular anchorages at La Cruz and Punta Mita, as well as two marinas in Nuevo Vallarta (upscale Paradise Village Marina and funky Marina Nuevo Vallarta) and one marina in Puerto Vallarta (Marina Vallarta). It's important to note that Puerto Vallarta and Nuevo Vallarta are in two different states (Jalisco and Nayarit respectively). Although they are also technically in two different time zones, all of Banderas Bay operates on PV (Central) time. Banderas Bay is a popular jumping off point for the "Puddle Jump" to the Marquesas and other South Pacific location, and therefore a popular provisioning location as well.

In the Puerto Vallarta area, it is possible to purchase almost anything you may need. However, like Cabo San Lucas, PV is a tourist area catering to gringos and prices tend to be higher than elsewhere in Mexico. Restaurants and other service businesses will frequently charge U.S. prices, quoted in dollars. A high percentage of the population speaks at least some English.

Buses and taxis are readily available. Within PV, buses cost 4.5 pesos. Buses to Nuevo Vallarta are around 15 pesos, and trips to La Cruz or Punta Mita are slightly higher. Taxis from the main grocery stores to Nuevo Vallarta are about 120–150 pesos. As in any other location in Mexico, ask the price before getting in a taxi.

Although there are small *tienda*s near each of the marinas or anchorages, the main grocery stores of interest to cruisers are Wal-Mart, Sam's Club, Commercial at Plaza Marina (walking distance from Marina Vallarta), and Mega-Commercial at Plaza Flamingo. All of these stores are along the main road into town from the marinas and anchorages. For cruisers at Paradise Village, Sunset Market in the Paradise Plaza mall is a convenient, though expensive, option. Wal-Mart, Commercial, and Mega-Commercial are all full-service grocery stores, carrying groceries, meats, good produce, and baked goods. Mega-Commercial has a small section containing Kirkland brand items from Costco. Many cruisers feel that Wal-Mart and Sam's have the best standard meats in town; however, Sam's Club sells meat in larger packages. Some cruisers buy a whole filet of beef from Sam's and cut it into thick steaks which can be individually packaged and frozen.

While Sam's Club is a membership warehouse, it is possible to get a free day pass at the membership desk that allows you to purchase items at 5% above the listed prices. In addition to good meats, canned goods, and other bulk items, Sam's Club carries a variety of gourmet and hard-to-find items, including Danish blue cheese, canned butter, smoked salmon, ricotta and shredded cheeses, and sliced pepperoni. Another interesting item we found was frozen mangoes, at 70–80 pesos per 3 kilogram bag.

Sunset Market (Paradise Village) caters to gringo tourists and has mix of reasonably priced Mexican products and very expensive imported U.S. products. When shopping there, it is important to check price labels unless you have a generous cruising budget. For example, some familiar cereals sold in Mexico (Frosted Flakes, etc.) were priced at 15–25 pesos per box while boxes of imported cereals (Great Grains granola, etc.) on the same shelf were priced at 65 –75 pesos. However, if you are looking for particular U.S. products and are willing to pay the price, Sunset Market is a good place to check.

Two other specialty stores in PV carry many hard-to-find items at high prices. One is GR (Guiterrez Rizo) Market, just across Isla Cuale in the Zona Romantica. Take any El Centro bus and get off at the first opportunity after the bridge that crosses the island. GR is about one block east (left) at the corner of Serdan and Constitucion. GR Market carries a large selection of Asian products; pickle relish, cranberry sauce, canned pumpkin, tomato paste, baking mixes and canned goods imported from the U.S.; Twinings teas; frozen phyllo dough and egg roll wrappers; and English language magazines. If you need nourishment before or after your shopping, the green building across the street sells excellent tacos.

Agro Gourmet is another high-end specialty store. Although they are primarily a restaurant supply business, they also sell direct to consumers. They have three locations: one in the Zona Romantica, one in Punta Mita, and one on the main road, one block toward town from Sam's Club. To find the store near Sam's Club, pass under an arch with the Agro Gourmet sign, adjacent to San Javier Marina Hospital. You may not immediately recognize that you are in a store since you walk in through the loading dock doors. Once inside, an English-speaking store assistant will greet you, carry your shopping basket, and otherwise help you with anything you need. Off the loading dock are a set of freezers with meats, cheeses, and prepared foods as well as a walk-in cooler full of specialty produce, including raspberries, spring salad mix, asparagus, and Portobello mushrooms. A side room has shelves of imported products, a nice selection of specialty oils and spices, Twinings teas, Asian products, cocktail sauce, and Cheez-Its. They even carry a selection of Norwegian "artisan waters" in beautiful bottles! Most of the prices are in the "if you have to ask…" range, but on a recent trip, we did buy some very nice sausages (Italian, breakfast, and kielbasa) for 165 pesos per kilo. I also indulged in some ridiculously expensive diet A&W root beer and diet Dr. Pepper. For those anchoring at Punta Mita, you can find a branch of Agro Gourmet near the El Anclote condominiums in a sand-colored, 3-story, palapa-topped building called P.O.S. (Plaza of Shops). If there is an American product you just have to have, Agro Gourmet will also special order items for cruisers or other seasonal residents. You can check them out on the internet at www.agro-gourmet.com.

For exceptionally good meats, many cruisers have discovered ComNor, which carries certified Angus beef and supplies restaurants in PV. It is on a side road across from Plaza Marina (first intersection toward town from the airport), just towards town from the Honda dealer. Walk one long block down the side road and you'll find ComNor. You don't have any sense that you are in a *carnecería*, as you won't find any meat in evidence! You walk into the front office, and a clerk will print out a price list for you. You let her know what you want, they'll gather your order in the back room and bring it out to you. Of most interest to cruisers are the meats sold by the portion *(porcionado)*. For example, ribeye and New York steaks of various grades are available in 10-, 12-, and 14-ounce portions, frozen and individually vacuum-sealed. Some products, such as boneless chicken breasts and hamburgers, are only available in 5- or 10-kilogram boxes. Good cuts of certified Angus beef ranged from 200–400 pesos per kilogram on a recent visit. As a special treat, we bought a one-kilogram package of two frenched racks of lamb for about 370 pesos.

Carne del Mundo in Bucerias also sells an interesting selection of meats and caters to cruisers. Selections include beef, sausages, ostrich, and chicken. They will freeze and vacuum-seal meats, and may offer free delivery for orders over 500 pesos. Carne del Mundo often posts information at the Vallarta Yacht Club in Paradise Village and other locations where cruisers congregate.

To resupply the liquor cabinet, check out Las Playas liquor store, ½ block toward town from Mega-Commercial for hard-to-find brands of liquor. For common items, all of the major grocery stores carry an excellent selection of rum, tequila, and brandy and a limited selection of other items.

While not a grocery store, Casa Lori in La Cruz provides catering service and will prepare, package, and freeze meals for passages. This could be especially convenient for those provisioning for the "Puddle Jump" or making other long passages.

MANZANILLO AREA (TENACATITA, BARRA DE NAVIDAD, MELAQUE, SANTIAGO BAY):

The local hailing channel is VHF-22 and the local net is at 9 a.m. daily. Tenacatita, Barra de Navidad, and Santiago Bay are the three main cruiser hang-outs in the Manzanillo area. This is a wonderful region for cruising, and each of the areas has services of interest to cruisers.

Tenacatita:

From the Tenacatita anchorage, there are two main provisioning options. The first is to take your dinghy up the Jungle River trip to the village of Playa Tenacatita. Here you will find restaurants for lunch, as well as a small *tienda* that carries a limited supply of produce, canned goods, basic supplies, and some refrigerated items. A truck with fresh tortillas visits the village each afternoon. If you don't want to take your dinghy up the river, you can also take your boat around to the anchorage off of Playa Tenacatita (also known as "the Aquarium") and dinghy ashore from there.

For a better selection of provisions, many cruisers visit La Manzanilla, the small town about 3 miles across the bay from the anchorage. In La Manzanilla there are a variety of small to medium size *tienda*s, *tortillerías*, *carnecerías*, and a bakery. I like the Fruitería Dalia for their excellent selection of produce, and Abarrotes Lidia for friendly service and a good selection of groceries and refrigerated items.

To get to La Manzanilla, you can take your dinghy for the three-mile trip, drive the big boat across and dinghy in, or you can take your dinghy ashore on the beach adjoining the inner anchorage, walk down the beach to the Blue Bay Hotel and catch a taxi. A taxi to La Manzanilla is about 300 pesos round trip for four people. The driver will drop you off and come back to get you (and his fee) in three hours. The main advantage of the taxi is that you avoid the sometimes-difficult beach landing in La Manzanilla and can stay for lunch at one of the good restaurants, like Martin's. The beach swell can be dangerous in the afternoon in La Manzanilla, so if you are going to make the trip ashore by dinghy it is best to go in the morning, preferably on a calm day. Many cruisers have taken waves over the bow of their dinghy when launching from the beach in big swells. It's always disappointing to watch your groceries bobbing around in the bottom of your dinghy!

Barra de Navidad:

Cruisers from Tenacatita also travel the 13 miles into Barra de Navidad for provisions, internet access, and to pick-up or drop off visitors. Good anchorage is available in the shallow lagoon. The entrance channel is deep, but narrow beyond the marina, so seek local knowledge before going into the anchorage. If nothing else, hail other anchored boats on Channel 22 for entrance information. The marina at the Grand Bay Hotel is quite nice, but also very expensive. Entrance to the marina is well-marked with buoys. Both the anchorage and the marina are separated by water from the town of

Barra de Navidad. The village of Colimilla is on the shores of the lagoon, just beyond the marina.

From the anchorage or the marina, you can get around by dinghy or by water taxi. If you are traveling to Barra de Navidad by dinghy, you can tie up at the Hotel Sands, which has a seawall with posts for tying up. Water taxis travel regularly between Barra de Navidad and the marina. To hail a water taxi from the lagoon, you can call "*Taxi Aquatico*" on Channel 23. Water taxi fares are about 20 pesos roundtrip from the marina and 25 pesos roundtrip from the lagoon.

Once in Barra de Navidad, you will find a variety of *tienda*s. The main street is Veracruz, and there you will find an ATM and several *tienda*s. The Fruitería Ixtapa generally has a good selection of produce and other items. You will also find one or two veggie trucks in town with an excellent selection of produce, as well as eggs and chicken. The veggie trucks generally show up between 11 a.m. and noon and remain in town until mid-afternoon. They aren't always in the same place, so you just have to walk around and look for them. On Veracruz near the cathedral square, or near the square by the ATM, are good places to look. You will find several fish stores *(pescaderías)* on the lagoon side of Veracruz. Our favorite is the fisherman's coop near the "big tree" at the corner of Veracruz and Sonora.

Some of the best provisioning in the area, however, is in the village of Colimilla. There you will find Maria's Tienda. Maria speaks excellent English and specializes in yacht provisioning. In her *tienda*, she carries items that gringo cruisers want, such as

The dinghy dock at Hotel Sands in Barra de Navidad is a convenient starting point for a provisioning expedition. Cruisers may also use the pool at the hotel in exchange for occasionally buying drinks or food at the restaurant.

frozen chicken breasts and bagels from Costco, tonic water, lunch meat, cheese, nice produce, baking mixes, and other specialty items. Maria can also take your propane tanks to be filled. She will take special orders and find anything that you need from the large stores in Manzanillo and Guadalajara. With advance arrangements, Maria will also deliver groceries to your boat by *panga*, which is wonderful when you are stocking up on soda, beer, and water! Generally, if we are traveling back and forth to Barra, we will leave a list with Maria and let her know when we'll be back. When we return to the area, she'll have our order filled and ready for us. She has done an excellent job of finding us good meats, and many hard-to-find items. Maria is sometimes away from her *tienda*, so it's a good idea to call her on VHF-77 to see if she's there before heading into Colimilla.

To find Maria's Tienda, tie up your dinghy on the beach next to the *panga* dock, at the end of the street between Restaurant Colimilla and Restaurant Lydia. Walk one block up the hill and turn right. The *tienda* is a half block on the right, next to the driveway for Fortino's restaurant. Maria's uncle has a good fish store nearby. You can either ask her for directions, or arrange to have her get shrimp or fish for you. The dorado is wonderful!

Another special find in Barra de Navidad is the French Baker. During the cruising season, he delivers fresh-baked croissants, baguettes, and individual pies by *panga* every morning to both the marina and the lagoon. Many cruisers await his daily arrival with great anticipation! The French Baker also has a small café on the ocean side of Legaspi, across from a large white hotel.

Cruisers also enjoy the cake stand in Barra de Navidad, just up from the water taxi dock, next to the public beach entrance arch and Popeye's restaurant. And along Veracruz, you will find a couple of places offering wonderful roasted or barbecued chickens with all the trimmings. You will also find a variety of vendors with carts or trays of food. We sometimes see a couple of enterprising young men with a mobile candy and snack store mounted on a couple of wheelbarrows.

Melaque:

Until the mid-90's, most cruisers in the area anchored off of Melaque. Now that the Barra de Navidad lagoon is accessible to cruisers, most opt to anchor there since Melaque has the reputation of being rolly and is nicknamed "Rocky Melaque". Some cruisers love Melaque, however, and you'll almost always see a few boats anchored there. You can also reach Melaque from Barra de Navidad by taking a 4 peso "chicken bus" or catching a taxi for about 50 pesos.

Melaque has more services than Barra de Navidad, including a Banamex bank and a number of hardware stores. There are many *tienda*s and *carnicerías*, but of particular interest to cruisers is "Super-Hawaii". This *tienda* specializes in gringo food. On a recent visit, I managed to stock up on many hard-to-find items including brown sugar, pickle relish, and Wheat Thins. Super-Hawaii also has good produce and a counter with cheese and other refrigerated items.

Maria welcomes a customer to her well-stocked *tienda* and yacht-provisioning business in Colimilla. She is happy to fill special orders, and makes regular trips to large stores in Manzanillo and Guadalajara.

The French Baker delivers pastries by *panga* to a cruiser in Barra de Navidad. Each morning, he bakes and delivers baguettes, croissants, filled croissants, and tarts. (Mike Clemens photo)

Santiago Bay:

From the anchorages in Santiago Bay or Las Hadas, it is an easy taxi or bus ride to the large grocery stores on the outskirts of Manzanillo, including Soriana and Commercial. From the west end of Santiago Bay (Playa Miramar or Boca Chica), a taxi ride to Soriana or Commercial is about 70 pesos. It is also possible to walk down Playa Mirimar to the main highway and catch a bus into Manzanillo. From Las Hadas, you can walk, bus, or taxi to the grocery stores. In 2004, some cruisers found Commercial to be dirty and preferred Soriana. Both stores have a full line of groceries, produce, deli items, baked goods, and sundries. For routine items, there is a small *tienda* near Playa Miramar on one of the streets perpendicular to the beach in the residential area.

ZIHUATENEJO AND IXTAPA:

The local hailing channel is VHF-22 and the local net is at 8:30 a.m. Zihuatenejo is a lovely town and a good place to provision. Most cruisers anchor out in the inner harbors (Municipal and Madero) or in the anchorage along Playa La Ropa. Even

A mobile candy and nut store balanced on a wheelbarrow attracts customers in Barra de Navidad. The young operators wheel their carts through the cobblestone streets, and weigh out portions on a balance scale.

from the outer reaches of La Ropa, the downtown dinghy landing is only 10 or 15 minutes away. Cruisers generally beach their dinghies near the Municipal Pier where there are often one or two men standing by to help you land and to watch over your dinghy. In past years, Rick of Rick's Bar has hired them during the evening hours to watch dinghies and they work for tips during the day.

Once ashore, you will find taxis standing by near the municipal pier. Commercial is about a 20-peso taxi ride away and is a large, well-stocked establishment. Downtown Zihuatenejo is compact and easily walkable and has one of my favorite municipal *mercados* in all of Mexico.

A good place to start out is Rick's Bar, which is the local cruisers hangout and information center. From the dinghy landing, turn right and walk along the waterfront until you reach the basketball court. Turn left and head inland about ½ block on Avenue Cuauhtemoc to Rick's. Once there you can pick up a map of downtown with places of interest to cruisers marked.

The central *mercado* is well-organized and filled with stands carrying meat, fish, produce, baked goods, canned goods, cheese, household goods, and clothing. Throughout the downtown area, you will find other small *tienda*s, *panaderías*, liquor stores, and stores carrying specialty items such as vanilla, honey, and coffee. Near the municipal pier are a number of stalls catering to cruise ship passengers. This is a good place to find the lovely, brightly-painted wooden bowls and platters found mainly in Zihuatenejo. These bowls and platters make beautiful and practical serving dishes to have aboard.

Another provisioning gem in Zihuatenejo is Ismael and his wife, Hilda. They will fill diesel jugs and propane tanks, arrange for laundry service, take away garbage, and deliver water, soda, beer, and soft drinks to your boat by *panga*. You can reach Ismael on VHF-65.

ACAPULCO:

The local hailing channel is VHF-68 and the local net is at 8:30 a.m. In recent years, Acapulco has been of more interest to sportfishers and mega-yachts than to cruisers. Since Marina Chahue opened at Huatulco, most cruisers opt to bypass Acapulco and instead head straight to Huatulco. However, Acapulco is the largest city on the southern coast of Mexico and has a variety of large stores for convenient provisioning.

Buses and taxis are available from the marinas and anchorages. Once in town, you will find a large WalMart, Sam's Club, Comercial Méxicana, and other large grocery stores with a full range of canned goods, sundries, bakeries, deli counters, and butchers. There is also a farmer's market about two blocks inland from Playa Hornos. Smaller *tienda*s are found within walking distance of the marinas.

Cruisers recommend that you do not use the Acapulco municipal water without heavy treatment, and that you do not use your watermaker within the harbor. Bottled water is readily available in all stores.

HUATULCO:

The anchorages around Huatulco and Marina Chahue have become the major jumping-off points for small vessels traveling south across the Gulf of Tehuantepec. Enrique, the manager of Marina Chahue, is extremely helpful to cruisers and knows where to find just about everything. From the anchorages or the marina, a taxi will

In Zihuatenejo, beautifully painted wooden bowls and platters are commonly available. These make attractive and durable serving dishes aboard boats, and are great gifts as well.

take cruisers to the town of La Crucecita for about 20 pesos. There are a variety of grocery stores and *tienda*s in this small town inhabited mainly by people who work in the beachfront hotels of Huatulco.

Cruisers mentioned that the new grocery store, La Fuenta, has all of the essentials as well as a nice deli counter, however the selection of produce was not as good as in other parts of Mexico. Just south of the main intersection in town, a prepared food supplier offers modestly-priced, frozen, vacuum-packed prawns, chicken, and other items. On the street bordering the central *mercado*, you will find a couple of *tienda*s that carry good produce. One block north of the central plaza, cruisers reported finding a very clean *carnecería*, commonly identified as the "air conditioned *carnecería*". There is a public market near the square that sells some interesting items, including soft cheeses flavored with the herb *epazote*; roasted crickets; dried chocolate tortillas; and ready-made *mole* sold in plastic bags.

SMALL VILLAGES ALONG THE WAY:

I haven't mentioned every place you are likely to find food in Mexico. Almost every small town or tourist area has a *tienda*. These may be very small with limited goods: frequently beer, a few canned goods, tortillas and perhaps a little produce. Most American kitchens have more food in them than the average small *tienda* in Mexico!

When shopping at small *tienda*s in Conception Bay, I've essentially bought out the whole produce section. The produce section in a small *tienda* may consist of a couple of potatoes and onions, a few limes, and perhaps a few tomatoes or bananas.

If you hang out in any area for awhile, check to see what day the local *tienda* receives supplies. For example, Bahia de Los Angeles has four *tienda*s and each one is supplied on a different day. By paying attention to the supply days, you have the best opportunity to get fresh produce and milk. In small communities, or areas populated by cruisers or RVers, also check to see if there are veggie trucks or seafood vendors that serve the area.

Appetizers, Beverages, and Raft-Up Food

A few good appetizer recipes are an important part of every cruising cook's repertoire. Wherever cruisers gather, food is an important part of the social scene, and frequently that means finger food. Following are some suggested recipes that make good additions to dinghy raft-ups, potlucks on the beach, or cocktail hour in the cockpit. Most of these recipes use ingredients that are readily available in Mexico.

TUNA PATE

This recipe can be made quickly, using ingredients that are easy to find in Mexico. I make this recipe if invited to drinks or a potluck on short notice.

Serves: 6

1—7 oz. can tuna, drained
1 tablespoon softened butter
½ cup heavy cream (*crema para batir*)
2 tablespoons capers, drained
1½ tablespoons parsley, minced
1 teaspoon lime or lemon rind, grated
1 teaspoon lime or lemon juice
salt and pepper to taste

In a bowl, mash the tuna and butter until smooth.

Beat the cream until it forms soft peaks and fold it into the tuna with the capers, parsley, lemon rind, lemon juice, salt, and pepper.

Pack into a crock or bowl and chill until ready to serve. Can be kept for 2–3 days. Serve with crackers or crostini.

DEVILED EGGS

Deviled eggs are always popular, and usually the first item to disappear at potlucks!

Makes: one dozen egg halves

7 large eggs
3 tablespoons mayonnaise
1 teaspoon Dijon mustard or grainy mustard
1½ teaspoons cider vinegar
3 drops hot sauce
¼ teaspoon Worcestershire sauce
pinch of cayenne (optional)
salt and pepper to taste

Place eggs in a medium saucepan, cover with one inch of water, and bring to a boil over high heat. Remove pan from heat, cover, and let stand for 12 minutes. Transfer the eggs to a bowl of cold water (ice water, if possible) and let sit for 5 minutes.

Carefully peel the hard-boiled eggs. Cut eggs in half lengthwise and scoop yolks into a small bowl. Mash egg yolks with a fork until no lumps remain. Add remaining ingredients, and mix with a rubber spatula, mashing mixture against the side of the bowl until smooth. Spoon yolk mixture into a Ziploc bag. If not serving immediately, store the Ziploc of yolk mixture and the egg white halves (in an airtight container) in the refrigerator.

Just before serving, arrange the 12 nicest looking egg white halves on a serving platter. Discard remaining egg white halves. Snip one corner off the Ziploc bag containing the yolk mixture. Gently squeeze the filling through the hole into the egg white halves. Garnish with paprika, sliced olives, or tiny shrimp.

ROLL-UPS

This deceptively simple appetizer is always a hit. The filling ingredients are variable and can be changed to match your mood and your larder.

tortillas
cream cheese
diced ham
diced green chiles
minced cilantro

Spread tortillas with cream cheese, then sprinkle with ham, chiles, and cilantro. Roll the tortilla into a tight cylinder, slice into rounds, and arrange on serving platter.

EASY MINI-QUICHES

These elegant mini-quiches are much easier than they look. Try them with any filling ingredients that you have available.

2 large eggs
1 cup milk
½ cup Bisquick
shredded cheese
fillings (ham, shrimp, salmon, green onions, etc.)

Blend the eggs, milk, and Bisquick in a food processor or blender along with shredded cheese and any other fillings (ham, shrimp, salmon, green onions, etc.).

Pour the batter into mini muffin tins. Bake at 400° until set, 15–20 minutes.

I have a small food processor aboard Legacy and find that a half recipe just fits in the food processor and fills one mini-muffin pan (12—2-inch quiches or 24—1½-inch quiches). My favorite variation is cream cheese and salmon quiches. For each batch, I add 1 oz. smoked salmon, 1 oz. cream cheese, and one minced scallion to one egg, ½ cup milk, and ¼ cup Bisquick.

RITA'S POTATO NACHOS

Serves: 6–8

2 large unpeeled baking potatoes, cut in $1/8$-inch thick slices
olive oil
salt and pepper
1 ½ cups grated cheese
1 tomato, seeded and chopped
1—4 oz. can diced green chiles
1—4 oz. can sliced black olives
1 small onion, finely chopped

Optional garnishes:
Sour cream or *crema*
Guacamole
Salsa
Chopped fresh cilantro

Preheat oven to 425°. Line a baking sheet with foil. Place potato slices in a single layer close together on the baking sheet. Brush the potatoes lightly with olive oil or spray with olive oil spray. Season with salt and pepper. Bake for 10 minutes.

Top the potatoes with cheese, tomato, chiles, olives, and onion and bake again until the potatoes are tender and the cheese is melted, about 8–10 minutes. Serve with desired garnishes.

NACHOS

Tortilla chips
Grated cheese (cheddar, *asadero*, *Chihuahua*, or Monterey jack)
1 can diced green chiles
chopped red onion (optional)
1 can sliced black olives (optional)
cooked ground beef (optional)

Preheat oven to 350°. Lightly oil a 9 × 13 inch baking pan. Place a single layer of tortilla chips on the bottom of the pan, sprinkle with grated cheese and chiles, as well as any of the desired optional ingredients. Continue layering tortilla chips and other ingredients until the pan is full or until you have enough to serve everyone. Bake the nachos in the oven for 10–15 minutes or until the cheese is melted and the chips are starting to brown. Serve warm with salsa, guacamole, refried beans, sour cream, or *crema*.

SEVEN-LAYER DIP

The most elegant presentation of this dip I ever saw was on Wind Jester. Our friend, Anne, found two medium-sized, fluted clear plastic bowls shaped like the tortilla "bowl" in which you sometimes see taco salads served. The layered ingredients were spectacular when highlighted in these bowls.

Serves: 10

1—16 oz. can refried beans
1—7 oz. can diced green chiles
1 cup thick and chunky prepared red salsa
2 cups prepared guacamole
1 cup shredded Cheddar cheese (substitute: Chihuahua or Manchego)
1 cup *crema* (substitute: sour cream, thinned with 2 tablespoons milk)
1—4-oz. can sliced black olives

Spread the beans evenly over the bottom of a shallow 1 ½ quart casserole or baking pan. Layer the chiles, salsa, guacamole, cheese, and *crema* on top of the beans. Scatter olives on top. Serve with tortilla chips for dipping.

Note: This is always a popular dish for cocktail hour or potlucks. It's not only delicious, but visually appealing as well.

JICAMA WITH CHILE AND LIME

1 large jicama
Juice of 1 or 2 limes
Mild chili powder, to taste

Peel the jicama and slice ¼-inch thick, or cut into ½-inch sticks. Arrange the slices or sticks attractively on a serving platter, sprinkle with lime juice, then sprinkle with chili powder to taste. This dish makes a refreshing addition to an appetizer buffet.

PICKLED CARROTS

Carrot sticks
2 tablespoons salt
1 teaspoon sugar
2 cloves garlic, peeled and sliced
2 teaspoons dill weed or seed
1 medium onion, sliced
1 cup water
1 cup vinegar

Fill quart jar with carrot sticks. Add salt, sugar, garlic, dill, and onion. Bring water and vinegar to a boil. Pour vinegar mixture over the carrots and rotate the jar to mix. Refrigerate for at least one day before serving.

PICKLED FISH IN MUSTARD DILL SAUCE

Sandy on Pegasus shared this recipe with me. When I made it for a potluck in La Paz, it was the hit of the party. It is also a good recipe to use if you catch a big fish that won't fit in your freezer.

1 kilo filet of dorado or other firm white fish

Pickling mixture:

3½ cups water
⅔ cup cider vinegar
1 tablespoon salt

Sauce:

3 tablespoons sugar
¼ cup water
1 tablespoon red wine vinegar
1 tablespoon cider vinegar
1 tablespoon salt
4 tablespoons Dijon mustard
¼ cup oil
1 teaspoon pepper
Dill to taste

Cut fish into thin slices or small chunks and place into airtight container. Combine water, vinegar, and salt to make pickling mixture, then pour over fish. Refrigerate overnight.

Drain pickling mixture off the fish. Mix sauce ingredients, then layer fish and sauce in an airtight container. Marinate in the refrigerator for 2–3 days. The pickled fish will keep, refrigerated, for 2–3 weeks.

GOAT CHEESE WITH MARINATED PEPPERS

1 yellow bell pepper
1 red bell pepper
3 poblano chiles
3 tablespoons olive oil
1 tablespoon white wine vinegar
2 cloves garlic, crushed with the flat of a knife blade
1 log of goat cheese (6—11 oz.)

Halve and seed the peppers. Grill (skin side down) or broil (skin side up) the pepper halves until the skins are charred, about 15 minutes. Remove peppers from the grill or oven, place peppers in a paper bag, close, and let steam for 15–20 minutes. Remove peppers from the bag, then slide off and discard the charred skins.

Dice the roasted peppers and place in a bowl with the oil, vinegar, and garlic. Cover the pepper mixture and chill for at least 8 hours for the flavors to develop.

To serve, bring the peppers to room temperature. Remove the garlic. Place the goat cheese log on a serving platter and spoon the peppers over it. Serve with crostini or crackers.

HOT CHEESE DIP

2 tablespoons butter
3 scallions, minced
2 jalapeños, minced
½ teaspoon ground cumin
¾ cup *crema* or sour cream
2 cups grated cheddar or Chihuahua cheese
green or red hot pepper sauce

Melt butter in a saucepan and add the scallions, jalapeños, and cumin. Cook, stirring frequently, over low heat for 7–8 minutes. Do not let the mixture brown.

Add the *crema* or sour cream and stir until warm. Add the cheese, stirring constantly until the cheese melts and mixture is smooth and glossy. Transfer the dip to a bowl, drizzle a little hot pepper sauce on top in an attractive pattern, and serve warm with crostini or tortilla chips. Makes 2 cups.

WARM ARTICHOKE AND CHILE DIP

Serves: 6

1—7 oz. can diced green chiles
1—14 oz. can artichoke hearts, drained, rinsed, and finely chopped
3 or 4 pickled jalapeños, seeded and minced (substitute: ½ teaspoon hot pepper sauce)
1 cup mayonnaise
1 cup (4 oz.) shredded Monterey Jack cheese (substitute: *Chihuahua* or *Manchego*)
⅓ cup grated Parmesan or Romano cheese (substitute: *anejo*)

Heat oven to 400°. Butter or oil a shallow 9-inch casserole dish or pie pan. Mix all ingredients together in a medium bowl. Spread mixture evenly in the prepared pan.

Bake 20 minutes, or until the cheese is melted and bubbly. Serve hot, directly from the baking dish, with tortilla chips, crostini, or thin slices of baguette.

SHRIMP BUTTER

Serves: 6

½ lb. medium shrimp, cooked, shelled, and deveined (substitute: canned shrimp)
3 oz. cream cheese, at room temperature
2 tablespoons butter, softened
2 small cloves garlic, minced
1 jalapeño, seeded and minced
2 tablespoons lime juice
¼ teaspoon salt

Chop shrimp into small bits. Combine shrimp in medium bowl with cream cheese, butter, garlic, jalapeño, lime juice, and salt. Mix well. Cover and refrigerate at least two hours. Can be made the day ahead. Serve with tortilla chips, crostini, or crackers.

SMOKED SALMON SPREAD

6 oz. cream cheese, at room temperature
4 oz. smoked salmon, flaked
2 tablespoons *crema* or sour cream
2–3 teaspoons lime juice
¼ teaspoon salt
white pepper (optional)
additional *crema* or sour cream for garnish
fresh dill (optional)

In a food processor or blender, process the cream cheese, salmon, *crema*, 2 teaspoons of the lime juice, and the salt for 30–45 seconds or until smooth. Taste and add more lime juice, salt, or white pepper if you like.

Transfer the spread to a small serving bowl, cover, and chill for 2 hours or overnight. Before serving, garnish with sour cream or *crema* and sprigs of fresh dill, if desired. Makes 1⅓ cups.

MEXICALI BEAN SPREAD

1 can kidney beans, rinsed and drained
3 tablespoons water
1 tablespoon tomato paste (substitute: ¼ cup *pure de tomate* for tomato paste and water)
1 tablespoon lime juice
1 teaspoon cumin
¾ teaspoon oregano
¼ teaspoon hot pepper sauce
1 pinch ground cinnamon

In a food processor or blender, process all ingredients for 1 minute or until smooth. Serve as an appetizer, accompanied by tortilla chips or pita bread, or make sandwiches with it, garnishing them with sliced cucumber and lettuce. Makes 1½ cups.

BOILED SHRIMP

Medium to large raw shrimp, ¼ kilo per person

Shell and devein medium to large shrimp. Bring a generous quantity of water to a rolling boil in a large pot. Add about 1 tablespoon of salt. Add shrimp and immediately set a timer. Starting at about 2 minutes, stir the shrimp each minute and check for doneness (2–5 minutes depending on quantity and size of shrimp). Shrimp are done when they are pink in color and firm to the touch. Do not overcook. When done, remove from water, rinse with cool water, and store them refrigerated or on ice until served. Serve with Garlic-Butter (page 178), Cocktail Sauce (page 178), or Pelagic's Diabla Sauce (page 178).

CHRIS' CROSTINI

1 or more stale thin baguettes
olive oil

Preheat oven to 350°. Slice baguettes into uniform slices a little less than ¼-inch (about ³⁄₁₆-inch) thick. Brush or spray both sides of each slice with olive oil and lay on a cookie sheet. Bake about 10 minutes until slices are golden brown. The slices brown more evenly if you turn them ⅔ of the way through the baking process. If the baked slices look dry, you can brush them with a little more olive oil. Let cool and serve with spreads or dips. Can be kept for up to two weeks in an airtight container or Ziploc bag. Crostini can be refreshed by re-baking for 4–5 minutes in a hot oven.

Note: When in Barra de Navidad, we buy extra baguettes from the French Baker to make crostini. Crostini make a nice change from crackers or tortilla chips with dips and other appetizers.

GUACAMOLE

Guacamole is a cruising staple in Mexico. In its simplest form, it is quick and easy to whip up a batch for an appetizer or to accompany dinner.

2–3 ripe avocados
juice of 2 small limes
¼ cup minced onion
2 cloves garlic, minced
Optional ingredients: minced jalapeños or serrano peppers, chopped tomatoes, minced cilantro.

Cut avocados in half, then remove pits and reserve. Holding an avocado half in your hand, mash the pulp with a fork, then scoop the mashed pulp into a small bowl. Add lime juice, minced onion, and minced garlic, and stir well. Add optional ingredients, if desired. Serve immediately, or store refrigerated in an airtight container. To reduce browning during storage, place the dip and the reserved pits into an airtight container without much extra space.

Note: If you add chopped tomatoes, add them just before serving. Guacamole with chopped tomatoes does not keep well.

SALSA FRESCA

3 large ripe tomatoes, chopped
½ medium onion, finely chopped
3 tablespoons fresh cilantro, minced
2–3 serrano or jalapeño peppers, seeded and minced
3 tablespoons lime juice
½ teaspoon salt

Combine all ingredients in a medium bowl. Cover and let stand about 15 minutes to blend flavors. Serve within a few hours.

CRANBERRY COOLER

Serves: 1

2 tablespoons unsweetened cranberry juice concentrate
1 oz. gin or vodka (optional)
1—12 oz. Seven-Up or Sprite (we prefer diet)
lime wedge

Pour unsweetened cranberry juice concentrate and gin or vodka, if using, into a tall glass over ice cubes (if available). Add diet Seven-Up or Sprite. Squeeze lime wedge into glass and serve.

Note: Unsweetened cranberry juice concentrate is found in the health food section of U.S. supermarkets in 8-ounce glass bottles. The brand I use is Knudsen. The opened bottle of concentrate keeps well in the fridge. This is one of our favorite beverages on the boat.

HIBISCUS *AGUA FRESCA*

Agua Frescas are refreshing, lightly sweetened beverages commonly seen in Mexico. Dried hibiscus flowers are known in Mexican markets as *jamaica* and can frequently be found in the produce section.

Serves: 6

½ cup dried hibiscus (*jamaica*) flowers
½ cup sugar
juice of two limes

Make hibiscus tea by steeping dried flowers in boiling water for about 10 minutes. Strain tea into a pitcher or beverage container.

Add sugar and lime juice then add cold water to make 2 quarts. Refrigerate and serve chilled.

MARGARITAS

Serves: 4–6

2 tablespoons grated lime zest
1 cup lime juice
½ cup *jarabe natural* (sugar syrup)
1 pinch salt
2 cups crushed ice
1 cup 100 percent *agave* tequila, preferably *reposado*
1 cup Triple Sec (substitute: *Controy*, a Mexican liqueur)

Combine lime zest and juice, *jarabe*, and salt in large liquid measuring cup, cover with plastic wrap and refrigerate until flavors meld, 4–24 hours.

Divide 1 cup crushed ice between 4 or 6 margarita glasses. Strain juice mixture into 1-quart pitcher or cocktail shaker. Add tequila, Triple Sec, and remaining crushed ice, stir or shake until thoroughly combined and chilled, 20–60 seconds. Strain into ice-filled glasses, serve immediately.

SUNBREAK MANGO MARGARITAS

Our friends, David and Leslie on SunBreak, serve these delicious and decadent margaritas.

Serves: 4

1 cup tequila
1 cup mango pulp, fresh, jarred, or canned; or 1 cup frozen mango halves
⅔ cup *jarabe natural* (clear sugar syrup)
⅓ cup water
ice cubes

Pour ingredients into ice-filled blender. Mix for 30 seconds to 1 minute. Serve immediately.

TEQUILA SUNRISE

Serves: 1

2 teaspoons grenadine syrup (*jarabe sabor granadina*)
3 tablespoons tequila
2 teaspoons lime juice
¼ cup orange juice

Fill cocktail glass ⅓ full with crushed ice or ice cubes (if available). Pour grenadine over ice. Without stirring, add tequila, lime juice, and orange juice. Serve at once.
Note: This is the specialty of the house for cocktail hour on Legacy.

SANGRIA

Serves: 4–6

1 liter red table wine
¼ cup brandy
½ cup orange juice
¼ cup *jarabe natural* (clear sugar syrup)
1 orange, sliced
2 limes, sliced
1 cup club soda or mineral water

In a large pitcher, combine all ingredients except club soda. Refrigerate for at least 30 minutes. Add the club soda just before serving.

Make-ahead Main Dishes

The following recipes all can be made ahead and then reheated for easy meals underway or on passages. On Legacy, we reheat meals underway in a small microwave using an inverter to generate 110-volt power. If you don't have a microwave available, warm main dishes on the stovetop, in the oven, or in a makeshift double boiler made of a metal mixing bowl set over a saucepan of simmering water.

CHICKEN TETRAZZINI

Serves: 6

8–12 oz. cooked chicken, shredded or diced
2 red bell peppers
6 tablespoons butter
6 tablespoons flour
2½ cups chicken broth
1 cup heavy cream (crema para batir)
salt
pepper, black
¼ teaspoon Tabasco or other hot pepper sauce
½ cup sherry
1 lb. spaghetti
¾ cup bread crumbs
½ cup Parmesan cheese, grated
2 tablespoons butter

Dice the red peppers. Melt the 6 tablespoons butter in a heavy saucepan, then stir in flour. When it is cooked and bubbling, stir in the chicken stock gradually, continuing to stir until the sauce is thickened. Add the cream and season with the salt, pepper, Tabasco, and sherry.

Add the chicken and diced peppers to the sauce. Cook and drain the spaghetti, then add to the warm sauce. Spread mixture in a buttered baking dish. Cover the top with bread crumbs and Parmesan cheese and dot with the remaining butter. Place in a 475° oven for a few minutes until the topping is glazed and bubbling.

CHICKEN AND RICE SKILLET

Serves: 4

1 lb. boneless chicken breast
salt and pepper
1 tablespoon olive or canola oil
½ lb. chorizo sausage
1 small onion, diced
1 red bell pepper, sliced
2 cloves garlic, minced
1 cup rice
2 cups chicken broth
1 cup chopped tomatoes
1 teaspoon cumin
1 teaspoon thyme
1 cup frozen peas
¼ cup sliced black olives

Cut the chicken breasts into ¼-inch slices, then sprinkle with salt and pepper. In a large nonstick skillet, heat the oil over moderate heat. Add the chicken breasts and chorizo and sauté, stirring frequently for 5 minutes or until lightly browned. Transfer to a plate.

Add the onion and red pepper to the skillet, sprinkle with salt and pepper and sauté, stirring, for 5 minutes or until softened. Add the garlic and rice and sauté, stirring, for 1 minute. Add the broth, tomatoes, cumin, and thyme and bring to a boil over high heat. Lower the heat and simmer, covered, for 15 minutes or until the rice is tender.

Add the peas, chicken, sausage, and olives to the skillet and mix well. Simmer for 5 minutes or until the peas are tender and the chicken and sausage are heated through. Good served with a green salad.

SHRIMP PAELLA

In addition to being a great dish to reheat for passage meals, this is an easy, never-fail hit for entertaining. We usually keep the ingredients on hand for impromptu company dinners.

Serves: 4

½ lb. chorizo
1 tablespoon olive oil
1 small onion, chopped
1 clove garlic, minced
1 can chicken broth
1 can diced tomatoes
½ teaspoon cinnamon
¼ teaspoon saffron threads, crumbled (optional, but a very nice touch)
1½ cups rice
½ lb. shrimp, shelled and deveined
1 cup frozen peas, thawed

Remove the chorizo from its casing. Over medium heat, cook the crumbled chorizo, onion, and garlic in hot oil until sausage is browned and onion is tender, about 5 minutes. Add broth, tomatoes and their liquid, cinnamon, saffron and rice. Heat to boiling. Cover and simmer 15 minutes. Add shrimp and peas; simmer 5 minutes more. Good served with crusty bread.

LINDA'S MILD JAMBALAYA

We like spicy foods such as Jambalaya. However, sometimes a milder version is appropriate. We find this to be the case on passages, where someone is always eating dinner then immediately going off-watch for a nap. Our good friend, Linda, introduced us to this mild version of Jambalaya.

Serves: 6

1 tablespoon canola or olive oil
1 large onion, chopped
1 lb. Polish kielbasa or other hard sausage, sliced
4 cups water
1—14-oz can diced tomatoes
1 package Zatarain's New Orleans-style Jambalaya mix
1 cup rice

Heat oil in heavy Dutch oven or large saucepan. Sauté chopped onions and sliced kielbasa in the oil until onions are soft. Add water and diced tomatoes, then bring to boil.

Add jambalaya mix and rice, and return mixture to boil. Reduce heat, stir, cover, and simmer over low heat for 25 minutes.

Remove from heat; let stand 5 minutes. Fluff and serve. Reheats well.

RIGATONI

Serves: 8

1 lb. rigatoni, cooked al dente
1 large onion, chopped
1 lb. lean ground beef
2 large jars pasta sauce
1 teaspoon cinnamon
1—15-oz. container ricotta cheese (substitute: *Panela*, *Queso Fresco*, or *Requeson*)
8 oz. shredded cheddar or mozzarella cheese (substitute: *Manchego* or *Chihuahua*)

While the rigatoni is cooking, sauté chopped onion and ground beef until the beef is browned. Add pasta sauce and ground cinnamon. Simmer about 15 minutes.

Cover bottom of 9 x 13 inch pan with sauce, add layer of rigatoni, cover with sauce, then dot with all of the ricotta cheese. Add another layer of rigatoni, a layer of sauce, then cover with shredded mozzarella or cheddar. Bake in 350° oven for 30–40 minutes. If cheese starts browning too much, cover loosely with foil.

Note: Rigatoni is a standard meal on races and cruises on Legacy. Made ahead and frozen or refrigerated, it can be rewarmed in the oven for a hearty meal underway. Reheated a second time it makes a great lunch.

HEATHER'S CHILI

This is a mild, not too acidic, chili that reheats well.

Serves: 4

1 large onion, chopped
¾ lb. lean ground beef
oil, if needed
3 cans diced tomatoes
2 cans kidney beans, drained
1 can tomato soup
2 tablespoons mild chili powder (more or less to taste)
1 tablespoon brown sugar or honey

Sauté chopped onion and ground beef together until beef is browned, using a little oil if beef is lean. Add diced tomatoes and their juice, along with drained beans and the can of tomato soup. Season with chili powder (add more to taste) and brown sugar. Simmer 30 minutes. Serve with cornbread.

CHRIS' PRESSURE COOKER BEEF STEW

Serves: 4

3 tablespoons olive oil
1 lb. stew beef, cubed
¾ cup flour
3 large onions, sliced
4 medium potatoes, cubed
3 medium carrots, sliced
1 bay leaf
1 cup red wine

Heat the oil in the bottom of the pressure cooker. Dredge the meat in the flour and sauté over high heat until lightly browned.

Add the sliced onions and sauté with the meat for a few minutes until the onions start to soften. Stir frequently to avoid burning, however a little crusting on the bottom of the pan will cook off later, adding flavor and color.

Add the potatoes, carrots, and any other vegetables to be included. Add the bay leaf and pour in the wine.

Seal the pressure cooker and bring up to pressure (high setting) and cook for 40 minutes. Remove from the heat and open the pressure cooker according to directions. Serve with hot biscuits or warm bread and the remainder of the bottle of wine. Excellent reheated on following days.

MACARONI BEEF CASSEROLE

This is comfort food, pure and simple, and a passage favorite on Legacy.

Serves: 4

1—12-oz. package macaroni or other pasta
1 tablespoon olive oil
1 large onion, diced
1 lb. ground beef
1 large jar pasta sauce
8 oz. shredded cheese, cheddar, *Manchego*, *Asadera*, or *Chihuahua*

Cook pasta al dente. Meanwhile, heat oil in a large saucepan. Sauté onion for about 5 minutes, then add ground beef and sauté until meat is browned. Add pasta sauce and simmer for 15 minutes. You can add additional seasoning at this point if you wish.

Drain pasta and add to the sauce. Mix well, then spread mixture in a 9 × 13 inch pan. Top with shredded cheese and bake in a 350° oven for 20 minutes or until cheese is melted and bubbly. Reheats well.

Note: Sometimes I'll put this casserole into two loaf pans instead of a 9 × 13 inch pan. I'll bake one initially, and refrigerate the other until needed.

SHEPARD'S PIE

Serves: 4

1 tablespoon oil
1 medium onion, diced
1 lb. ground beef
2 tablespoons flour
1 ½ cups beef broth or bouillon
1 teaspoon oregano
1 can mixed vegetables (*ensalada de legumbres*), drained
3 cups mashed potatoes, homemade or 6 portions prepared from mix
½ cup grated cheese (Parmesan or anything else you have)

Heat oil in a large skillet. Add the onion and cook for 2–3 minutes. Break up and add ground beef. Cook, stirring occasionally, until beef is well-browned. Sprinkle flour onto the beef and stir. Cook for about 2 minutes, then add the beef broth and oregano. Bring to a simmer and cook, stirring, until the sauce thickens. Add drained vegetables and remove from heat.

Pour beef mixture into 9-inch square pan. Top with prepared mashed potatoes and grated cheese. Bake in 350° oven for 30 minutes until top is browned and mixture is hot through.

QUICHE LORRAINE

Serves: 4–6

1—9-inch pie crust (see page 164)
3 large eggs, lightly beaten
1 ½ cups heavy cream or half & half
½ teaspoon salt
¼ teaspoon ground black pepper
pinch of nutmeg
1 cup chopped, cooked bacon
1 cup grated Swiss, *Chihuahua*, or other mild cheese

Preheat oven to 375°. Place crust in 9-inch pie pan.

Beat together the eggs, cream, salt, pepper, and nutmeg. Arrange the bacon and cheese in the bottom of the pastry shell. Pour the custard over the bacon and cheese. Bake until the filling is browned and set, 25–35 minutes. Remove quiche from oven and allow to stand for 10 minutes. Serve warm or cold.

MACARONI AND CHEESE

Serves: 6–8

Bread Crumb Topping (optional):
6 slices good-quality white bread
3 tablespoons cold butter

Pasta and Cheese:
1 lb. elbow macaroni
1 tablespoon salt
5 tablespoons butter
6 tablespoons flour
1½ teaspoons dry mustard
¼ teaspoon cayenne
5 cups milk
8 oz. shredded Monterey Jack
8 oz. sharp cheddar (substitute for the two cheeses: a combination of *Manchego*, *Chihuahua*, *Asadero*, or other melting cheeses)
1 teaspoon salt

If using topping, tear the bread into rough pieces. Pulse the bread and butter in a food processor until crumbs are no larger than ⅛-inch. Set aside.

Bring a large saucepan or Dutch oven of water to a boil and add 1 tablespoon salt. Cook pasta until it is tender, not al dente. Drain pasta and set aside.

In now-empty saucepan, heat butter over medium-high heat until foaming. Add flour, dry mustard, and cayenne and whisk well to combine. Cook for about 1 minute, whisking constantly. Gradually whisk in the milk and bring mixture to a boil, whisking constantly. Reduce heat to medium and simmer, whisking occasionally, until sauce is thickened, about 5 minutes. Remove the sauce from heat and add the cheeses and 1 teaspoon salt, whisking until cheese is fully melted. Add pasta to the sauce and simmer over low heat, stirring constantly, until mixture is heated through.

If using topping, transfer mixture to a 9 × 13 inch pan and sprinkle evenly with bread crumbs. Broil until the crumbs are deep golden brown, 3–5 minutes, rotating pan if necessary for even browning. Remove from broiler and let stand for about 5 minutes, then serve.

MEATLESS TAMALE PIE

Serves: 6

Filling:
1 small onion, diced
2 cloves garlic, minced
2 medium green bell peppers, diced
1 tablespoon canola oil
2 tablespoons tomato paste
1 heaping teaspoon chili powder
½ cup water
3 cups kidney beans, mashed
¼ cup sliced green olives
3 tablespoons parsley, minced
freshly ground black pepper

Crust:
1 cup cornmeal
1 tablespoon flour
¼ teaspoon salt
1½ teaspoons baking powder
1 large egg, lightly beaten
½ cup milk
2 tablespoons canola oil
2 tablespoons diced green chiles

Topping:
½ cup shredded cheddar cheese (substitute: *Manchego* or *Chihuahua*)

Sauté the onions, garlic, and green pepper in the oil in a large nonstick skillet until the vegetables are softened (you may cover the skillet for a few minutes). Stir in the tomato paste and chili powder, then add the water, beans, olives, parsley, and pepper. Simmer the mixture, stirring it, until it is heated through.

Grease an 8-inch baking dish or shallow casserole, and spread the bean mixture in it evenly.

In a medium bowl, combine the cornmeal, flour, salt, and baking powder. Add the egg, milk, oil, and green chiles, and stir the mixture until just combined. Spread the batter over the bean mixture, top with the cheese, and bake the pie, uncovered, at 400° for 20 minutes or until the dough rises and is golden brown.

Note: This is a healthy and delicious alternative to high-fat tamale or taco casseroles.

VEGETARIAN SHEPARD'S PIE

1½ cups canned black beans, rinsed and drained
1 cup tomato sauce
2 tablespoons tomato paste
1 medium onion, chopped
¼ teaspoon oregano
¼ cup water
¾ teaspoon salt
pepper to taste
1 lb. potatoes, peeled, boiled, and mashed
½ cup mozzarella or *Oaxaca* cheese, shredded
2 tablespoons sour cream or *crema*
1 tablespoon butter, softened

In a medium saucepan, stir together the beans, tomato sauce and paste, onion, oregano, water, ¼ teaspoon of salt, and pepper to taste, and bring to a boil over medium heat. Reduce the heat, cover and simmer 20 minutes, or until the liquid is thickened and the onions are translucent. Spread the mixture in a shallow 1½-quart casserole and set aside to cool.

Preheat oven to 350°. Place the mashed potatoes in a large bowl. Add the mozzarella, sour cream, butter, the remaining ½ teaspoon salt and pepper to taste, and beat until well blended. Spread the potato mixture evenly over the beans. Score the potato topping with a fork and bake the pie for 45 minutes, or until the topping is bubbly and golden.

Other Favorite Main Dish Recipes

CHICKEN QUESADILLLAS

Serves: 4

1 tablespoon vegetable oil
1 red onion, sliced
1 green pepper, sliced
1 red pepper, sliced
6 oz. diced cooked chicken
8 oz. or so shredded cheese, cheddar or Monterey jack (substitute: *asadero* or *Chihuahua*)
6 to 8 flour tortillas

Cook sliced red onion in oil in medium saucepan for 3 minutes; add sliced peppers. Cook until nearly soft. Add cooked chicken and cook for another 3 minutes. Remove from heat and let stand for at least 15 minutes.

Sprinkle light layer of cheese over half of one tortilla. Top with thin layer of chicken mixture. Top with more shredded cheese. Fold tortilla in half to cover toppings.

Cook quesadilla in skillet over medium-high heat until cheese is melted and both sides are lightly browned. Cut into wedges and keep warm on plate in 200° oven while you cook the rest of the quesadillas. Serve with salsa or guacamole.

Note: In the States, I use refrigerated grilled chicken strips. In Mexico, I buy roasted chickens, pull the meat off the bones and freeze in meal-size pouches for use in this and other recipes.

CHICKEN BURRITOS

Serves: 4

1 tablespoon canola oil
1 lb. boneless chicken thigh, cubed
1 large onion, chopped
3 cloves garlic, minced
2 tablespoons flour
2 teaspoons chili powder
1 teaspoon cumin
½ cup chicken broth
1 cup buttermilk (substitute: sour cream or *crema*)
1—4-oz. can diced green chiles, drained
2 teaspoons tomato paste
8 flour tortillas

Preheat oven to 375°. In a heavy skillet, heat the oil over moderate heat. Add the chicken and cook until no longer pink. Using a slotted spoon, transfer the chicken to a bowl. In the same skillet, cook the onion and garlic uncovered until soft, about 5 minutes. Blend in the flour, chili powder, and cumin, and cook, stirring constantly, for 2 minutes.

Stir in the chicken broth, buttermilk, chilies, and tomato paste. Reduce heat to low and simmer, uncovered, for 4–5 minutes or until slightly thickened. Return the chicken to the skillet and stir.

Place a scant ½ cup of the chicken mixture on the lower third of each tortilla and roll it up. Place seam side down in an ungreased 9 x 13 inch baking pan and drizzle any remaining filling down the center. Bake, uncovered, for 5 minutes.

POACHED CHICKEN WITH AVOCADO SAUCE

This dish is nice on extra-hot days—poach the chicken in the morning while the temperatures are cooler, then make the avocado sauce just before serving.

Serves: 4

Poached chicken:
1 small onion, halved
2 bay leaves
8 black peppercorns
¼ teaspoon salt
1 lb. boneless, skinless chicken breast

Avocado sauce:
1 avocado
¼ cup plain yogurt or *crema*
2 tablespoons chives, chopped
2 tablespoons reserved poaching water
1 tablespoon lime or lemon juice
⅛ teaspoon salt
¼ teaspoon Tabasco or other hot pepper sauce

Place onion, bay leaves, peppercorns, and salt in a 12-inch skillet, add 2 inches of water, and bring just to a simmer. Add the chicken, cover, and cook over low heat for 8–10 minutes or until the juices run clear when pricked with a fork. Set aside 2 tablespoons of the poaching water for the sauce. Transfer chicken to a bowl, add enough of the poaching water to cover, and let cool to room temperature. Cover with plastic wrap and refrigerate until ready to serve.

Just before serving, prepare the avocado sauce: In food processor or blender, process the avocado, yogurt, chives, reserved poaching water, lime or lemon juice, salt, and Tabasco for 30 seconds or until smooth. Serve the chicken breasts whole or attractively sliced on the diagonal with 2 tablespoons of the avocado sauce spooned over each serving. Garnish with additional chives, if desired. Pass the remaining sauce on the side.

CHICKEN WITH SOUR CREAM AND MANGO CHUTNEY

Serves: 4

4 boneless, skinless chicken breasts
½ cup mayonnaise
½ cup sour cream or *crema*
2 tablespoons mango chutney
1 teaspoon curry powder
juice of 1 lemon or two small limes
fresh ground black pepper

Preheat oven to 450°. Lay chicken in a roasting dish. In a small bowl, whisk together mayo and sour cream. Add chutney and curry powder and whisk until smooth. Add lemon juice a little at a time to taste. Spoon sauce over chicken. Place in oven and roast until chicken is just cooked through, about 15 minutes. Grind fresh pepper over top and serve.

MILK-BRAISED CHICKEN

Serves: 4

oil
4 servings chicken pieces (breasts, thighs, drumsticks), bone in
1 quart whole milk (I use 1 liter aseptic packaged milk)
salt and pepper

Pour enough oil into the bottom of a large pot and heat over medium-high heat. Brown the chicken until it is a deep golden brown. Pour off excess oil if desired. Add enough milk to cover the chicken. Salt & pepper generously as these are the only seasonings. Simmer at low heat, uncovered, until the chicken is fork-tender, its juices run clear, and the liquid cooks down nearly to gravy. Tasty served over rice.

CHICKEN DINNER IN A DISH

This is an easy dish to put together underway. On a long day, it is great to stick this in the oven a few miles out of the anchorage so that it will be ready as soon as the anchor is down.

Serves: 4

4 boneless chicken breast halves
2 medium potatoes, quartered
2 carrots, cut into 1-inch pieces
1 large onion, cut into wedges
½ cup dry white wine or chicken broth
1 bay leaf
1 can green beans, drained

Preheat oven to 350°. In baking dish, arrange chicken, potatoes, carrots, and onion. Pour wine or chicken broth over the chicken and add bay leaf. Cover with foil and bake for 1 hour. Add green beans and continue baking for 10–15 minutes. Remove bay leaf and serve.

PASTA SALAD

Pasta salads are wonderful when the temperature rises. Cook the pasta and mix with the dressing ingredients in the morning; refrigerate the pasta until afternoon, then add remaining ingredients just before serving.

Serves: 2–4

8 oz. macaroni, fusilli or other pasta, cooked
3 tablespoons olive oil
3 tablespoons white wine vinegar
2 tablespoons chicken broth
salt and pepper to taste
8 oz. cooked chicken, diced
½ cup red onion, diced
1 ripe avocado, diced
3 medium tomatoes, seeded and chopped
2 cloves garlic, minced

Combine pasta, oil, vinegar, chicken broth, salt, and pepper in a large bowl while the pasta is still warm. Let cool to room temperature. Refrigerate, if you aren't going to serve immediately.

Stir in remaining ingredients. Taste and adjust the seasonings. Serve at room temperature.

Note: This recipe is just a starting point. Experiment with other leftover poultry, meat, or shrimp. Add whatever interesting vegetables or seasonings you have available. If you have cilantro, parsley, or fresh herbs available, they make a nice addition.

CHICKEN WITH ALMONDS (*POLLO ALMENDRADO*)

Serves: 2–4

2–4 boneless, skinless chicken breasts
3 tablespoons flour
½ teaspoon salt
3 tablespoons olive oil
1 recipe Easy Almond Sauce (page 173)

Lightly flatten chicken breasts to even thickness. Mix flour and salt, then dust chicken pieces with the flour mixture.

Heat oil over medium heat in large skillet. Add chicken and cook until lightly browned on both sides and cooked through, but still moist, about 6–7 minutes total.

Top with almond sauce and serve immediately with rice and veggies.

Note: Chicken cooked by this method can be served with any of the easy *crema* sauces found on page 173.

EASY CHICKEN *MOLE*

Serves: 4

1 tablespoon olive oil
4 boneless, skinless chicken breast halves
1—125-gram jar of *mole* paste
1—14 oz. can chicken broth

Heat oil in large nonstick skillet over medium-high heat. Add chicken breasts and brown about 2 minutes on each side. Remove from pan and keep warm.

Reduce heat to medium and add oil from top of *mole* paste to the skillet. Heat until warm, then add the rest of the *mole* paste. Cook, stirring constantly, until the paste is warm and smooth. Gradually stir in chicken broth until the sauce is smooth and thick. Heat to a low simmer.

Return browned chicken breasts to the skillet and spoon sauce over the top. Cover and reduce heat to low. Simmer until breasts are cooked through, about 10 minutes. Serve chicken breasts with *mole* sauce, rice, and vegetables.

TURKEY SCALOPPINI WITH CRANBERRIES

I included this recipe even though fresh cranberries are very difficult to find in Mexico. If you should somehow find that you have some fresh cranberries in your freezer, this makes an elegant, colorful, and easy holiday meal!

Serves: 6

2 lb. boneless, skinless turkey breast (substitute: chicken breast)
⅓ cup flour, seasoned with salt and pepper
3 tablespoons butter
6 tablespoons dry white wine
3 tablespoons raspberry vinegar (substitute: white wine vinegar)
¾ cup heavy cream
1½ cups raw cranberries
salt and pepper as needed

Slice turkey breast almost horizontally into small thin steaks or scaloppini, 2–3 inches in diameter and ½-inch thick. Lightly dredge each one in flour and set aside.

In a large pan, melt 2 tablespoons butter over medium-high heat. When foam is beginning to subside, add several pieces of turkey and cook quickly on both sides just until sealed, but not cooked through. Remove from heat and keep warm while cooking remaining turkey. Add additional butter as needed, letting it get hot before adding more turkey.

Return all turkey to pan and add white wine and vinegar. When it bubbles, add cream. Bring almost to a boil and reduce heat. Add cranberries and simmer gently, uncovered, until turkey is cooked through, 3–5 minutes. Remove scaloppini and arrange on serving platter.

Increase heat, stir, and let cranberries and cream bubble until sauce thickens slightly and is a light pink color. Taste it and adjust seasoning with salt and pepper. Pour sauce over turkey and serve immediately with hot rice or buttered noodles.

EASY BAJA-STYLE FISH TACOS

Serves: 2

8 oz. filet of white fish
1 teaspoon flour
1 teaspoon cornmeal
½ teaspoon chili powder
¼ teaspoon salt.
2 tablespoons olive oil
¼ cup mayonnaise
2 tablespoons prepared salsa
finely shredded cabbage (optional)
corn or flour tortillas, warmed
lime wedges

Cut fish filet into strips. In a small bowl, combine flour, cornmeal, chili powder, and salt. Mix well. Dust fish pieces with flour mixture.

Heat oil over medium heat in nonstick skillet. Add fish and fry 1 minute on each side, or until lightly browned outside and opaque to center. Drain on paper towels.

In a small bowl, mix mayonnaise and salsa. Serve fried fish immediately with tortillas, shredded cabbage, salsa mixture, lime wedges, and any other desired toppings.

FISH WITH GARLIC SAUCE

Serves: 2–4

2–4 filets of sea bass or other firm white fish
salt and pepper
3 tablespoons flour
1 tablespoon butter
2 tablespoons canola or olive oil
1 recipe Easy Garlic Sauce (page 173)

Season filets with salt and pepper, then dust with flour to coat. Shake off excess.

In a large skillet, heat butter and oil over medium heat. When butter begins to sizzle, add the fish and cook, turning once, until lightly browned outside and opaque throughout, about 3 minutes on each side.

Serve immediately with garlic sauce or any of the other easy *crema* sauces on page 173.

GRILLED FISH

Thick filets of firm white fish, such as dorado

The two secrets to successfully grilling fish are to use thick filets or steaks, and to carefully check for doneness, using an instant read thermometer if possible. Thin filets are better sautéed or broiled because it is too easy to overcook them on a hot grill.

Place fish on hot grill, skin side down (if applicable). Thick pieces should be turned once; for thinner pieces, cover the grill and don't turn them. Total cooking time will be 6–9 minutes per inch, but start checking for doneness early. Fish is done when it is opaque throughout. Use a sharp knife to make a small slit to check and remove from grill just before it is completely opaque since it will continue to cook off the grill. Using an instant read thermometer, most fish is done at 133–137°. For tuna and other fish served rare, the appropriate temperature is 120–125°.

CURRIED SHRIMP SALAD

Serves: 2

Dressing:
1 teaspoon canola oil
1 teaspoon curry powder
½ teaspoon minced ginger root
⅓ cup plain yogurt (substitute: *crema*)

Salad:
1 cup cooked shrimp, chopped
½ cup raisins
¼ cup chopped cashews
pepper, black
¼ cup chopped scallions

In a small skillet, heat the oil over medium heat, add the curry powder, and cook the mixture for about 30 seconds to eliminate the "raw" taste of the curry. Then in a medium bowl, mix the curry powder and oil with the ginger and the yogurt.

Add the shrimp, raisins, cashews, pepper, and 2 tablespoons of the scallions. Toss the ingredients to combine them thoroughly. Before serving, bring the salad to room temperature, and garnish it with the remaining 2 tablespoons of scallions.

JILL'S SHRIMP AND FETA POTLUCK SALAD

1 lb. rigatoni or penne pasta
1 large sweet onion, chopped
2 tablespoons olive oil
4 cloves garlic, minced
1 lb. feta cheese, crumbled (substitute: *panela* or *queso fresco*)
1 lb. shrimp, cooked
Freshly grated Parmesan or Romano cheese

Optional additions:
Chopped tomatoes
Salami
Red onion

Cook and drain the pasta. Cook the diced onion in olive oil. When nearly done, add garlic and cook, being careful not to brown the garlic. Add the crumbled feta and let it melt some. Add the cooked shrimp to warm. Pour shrimp mixture over pasta and combine. Stir in optional additions, as desired, and top with lots of freshly grated Parmesan or Romano cheese. Can be served warm, cold, or room temperature.

SAUTÉED SHRIMP

Serves: 4

1 ½ lb. large shrimp, peeled and deveined
½ cup olive oil
2 cloves garlic, minced
¼ cup fresh parsley, minced
1 clove garlic, minced
1 tablespoon lime or lemon juice
additional minced fresh parsley

Rinse and pat dry the shrimp. Combine olive oil and 2 cloves minced garlic in a large skillet. Don't skimp on the olive oil. Cook, stirring occasionally, over low heat until the garlic is golden, about 10 minutes; do not rush it. Increase the heat to medium-high and add the shrimp. Cook until they turn pink on the bottom, then turn them over.

Add parsley and additional minced garlic. Cook until the shrimp are firm and pink, about 5 minutes total. Sprinkle with lime or lemon juice and minced parsley.

Note: Shrimp are readily available and relatively inexpensive throughout the coastal areas of Mexico. Frequently, I'll clean and sauté an entire kilo of shrimp, then freeze the leftovers for use in shrimp tacos.

GRILLED SESAME SHRIMP

Serves: 4

1 lb. medium to large shrimp, shelled and deveined
1½ tablespoons soy sauce
1 tablespoon lime juice
1 tablespoon sesame oil (see Substitutions chapter)
½ teaspoon minced fresh ginger root
½ teaspoon cumin
2 teaspoons sesame seeds

Thread the shrimp on skewers, pushing the skewer through both ends of each shrimp. Place skewers on baking sheet, cutting board, or foil.

In a small bowl, combine soy sauce, lime juice, sesame oil, ginger, and cumin. Brush the mixture over both sides of the shrimp, then sprinkle with the sesame seeds.

Grill the shrimp for 2–4 minutes, turning once, or until just opaque. Push the shrimp off the skewers, divide among 4 plates, and serve immediately.

SHRIMP-STUFFED AVOCADOS

This elegant and delicious cold dish can be made with whatever raw vegetables you have available. The popular Aguacate Popeye, served at Restaurant Popeye in Barra de Navidad, is made with a salad mix of shredded lettuce, shredded carrots, and sliced radishes.

Serves: 2 as a main course, 4 as an appetizer

½ lb. cooked shrimp
1 tablespoon lime juice
2 tablespoons minced onion
¼ cup minced celery
¼ cup shredded carrot
¼–½ cup mayonnaise
2 large, ripe avocados

Unless shrimp are small, chop them into ½-inch pieces. Toss with lime juice. Add onion, celery, carrot, and toss to combine. Stir in mayonnaise to desired consistency. Halve the avocados and remove pits. Using a large spoon, carefully separate the avocado flesh from the skin, keeping it intact, then return the flesh to the avocado half. Place on plates (1 half for an appetizer, 2 halves for a main course) and fill with the shrimp mixture. Serve immediately.

FAJITAS WITH CILANTRO CREAM

In Mexico, flank steak is readily available and will sometimes be labeled *arrachera*. When in doubt, ask if the *arrachera* is already marinated. For this recipe, you want plain flank steak.

Serves: 4

Marinated beef:
½ cup lime juice
¼ cup cilantro, chopped
2 cloves garlic, minced
2 teaspoons cumin
1 lb. flank steak

Cilantro cream:
1 cup sour cream or *crema*
½ cup cilantro, chopped
½ teaspoon grated lime rind

Grilled vegetables:
1 red pepper, halved and seeded
1 green pepper, halved and seeded
1 onion, quartered
8 flour tortillas, warmed

Avocado salsa:
1 diced avocado
1 cup prepared salsa

To make the beef marinade: In a large baking dish, mix the lime juice, ½ cup cilantro, garlic, and cumin. Add the steak and turn to coat both sides. Allow the steak to marinate for 15 minutes. Grill the steak for 2–3 minutes per side for rare beef. Slice the steak on the diagonal.

To make the cilantro cream: In a blender or small food processor, combine the sour cream, remaining ½ cup cilantro, and lime rind. Blend until smooth, stopping to scrape down the sides. Serve with the fajitas.

To prepare the vegetables: Grill the red pepper, green pepper, and onion on the grill or under the broiler for 10–15 minutes, or until browned. Slice them into thin strips and combine.

Combine the diced avocado and the prepared salsa.

To serve, top the flank steak with the grilled vegetables. Let each diner place this mixture in the tortillas, top it with cilantro cream and avocado salsa, fold the bottom of the tortilla up and roll the sides in.

ARRACHERA

Most large grocery stores and many small ones carry marinated flank steak called *arrachera*. It makes wonderful and easy fajitas or tacos.

Serves: 4

1 tablespoon olive oil
2 large onions, sliced thin
1—600-gram package of *arrachera*
grilled bell peppers (optional)
Pickled Onions (page 179)
warmed flour or corn tortillas
other toppings as desired: salsa, guacamole, *crema*, chopped tomatoes, etc.

Heat oil in skillet over medium-low heat. Add onion slices and cook slowly, stirring frequently, until onion is limp, brown, and nicely caramelized. Set aside.

Cook *arrachera* by one of the following two methods: 1) Grill on hot fire to desired level of doneness. Allow to stand briefly, then chop into bite-size pieces. 2) Chop *arrachera* into bite-size pieces, then sauté in skillet with 1 tablespoon oil to desired level of doneness.

Place meat, vegetables, tortillas, and toppings on the table and let diners assemble their own creations.

BASIC GROUND BEEF TACOS

Serves: 2–4

2 teaspoons olive oil
1 medium onion, finely chopped
3 cloves garlic, minced
1 lb. ground beef
½ teaspoon oregano
½ teaspoon red pepper flakes
¼ teaspoon salt
½ cup dry red wine
warmed corn or flour tortillas
assorted toppings as desired: chopped tomatoes, shredded lettuce, shredded cheese, salsa, guacamole, *crema*.

Heat oil over medium heat in a skillet. Add the onions and garlic, and sauté until the onion softens, about 5 minutes.

Add the ground beef, oregano, red pepper flakes, and salt. Cook, stirring occasionally, until the meat is browned, about 5 minutes. Add the wine and continue cooking until most of the liquid evaporates, about 10 minutes.

Place meat, tortillas, and toppings on the table and let diners assemble their own tacos.

LA MANZANILLA JOE

Provisioning in Mexico, we've learned to take advantage of any unexpected ingredients that come our way. On one provisioning trip from Tenacatita to La Manzanilla we found a bag of prewashed spinach. My husband, Chris, invented this dish—reminiscent of Broadway Joe and Ukranian Joe that he'd eaten at Thirteen Coins restaurant in Seattle—to take advantage of the find.

Serves: 2–4

1 medium onion, chopped
3 cloves garlic, minced
1–2 tablespoons olive oil
½ lb. ground beef
½ bag prewashed spinach, stemmed and chopped
4–6 eggs
1½ tablespoons Bisquick (optional)
½ cup grated Parmesan
sour cream or *crema*

Preheat oven to 350°. Saute onion and garlic in olive oil in an ovenproof skillet until translucent. Add crumbled ground beef and cook until nearly done. Pour off excess fat. Add spinach and cook about 2 minutes until spinach is limp but still bright green.

Beat eggs lightly with Bisquick, if using, and pour over meat mixture. Sprinkle with grated Parmesan. Stick skillet into preheated oven and either bake for 10 minutes, or bake for 5 minutes then broil for five minutes, until eggs are set and cheese is browned. Serve topped with sour cream or *crema*.

Note: If you don't have an ovenproof skillet, you can cover the skillet and cook on the stovetop until the eggs are set.

PICADILLO

1 lb. ground beef
1 clove garlic, minced
oil, if needed
1 green pepper, chopped
½ cup dry red wine
½ cup raisins
½ cup chopped onion
1 bay leaf
½ teaspoon allspice
dash cayenne pepper
2 tomatoes, cut in wedges
¼ cup slivered almonds, toasted

Brown the ground beef with garlic, using a little oil if beef is lean. Stir in green pepper, wine, raisins, onion, bay leaf, allspice, and cayenne pepper. Simmer uncovered 20–25 minutes. Add tomato wedges and cook an additional 5 minutes. Remove bay leaf. Serve over hot rice, sprinkled with almonds.

LAMB FAJITAS WITH TEQUILA-LIME SAUCE

Serves 3–4

1½ lb. boneless lamb, cut ¼–½-inch thick

Marinade:
1 jalapeño, seeded and minced
2 cloves garlic, minced
¼ cup cilantro, coarsely chopped
2 teaspoons *achiote* paste (found in most Mexican grocery stores)
pinch of ground cloves or cinnamon
½ cup beer, preferably amber

Toppings:
Spinach or watercress, stems removed
¼ cup toasted slivered almonds
¾ cup chopped black olives
Tequila-Lime Sauce (page 174)
warmed flour or corn tortillas

Mix marinade ingredients in nonreactive dish or bowl. Place lamb in the marinade and turn pieces to coat all sides. Cover and refrigerate for several hours or overnight, turning once or twice.

Remove lamb from marinade, and salt meat on both sides (if desired). Place on hot grill and cook for 3–5 minutes per side, to desired level of doneness. Remove lamb to a plate or platter and set aside for 5–10 minutes.

Cut the lamb crosswise into thin strips. Place in serving bowl on the table along with tortillas, toppings, and Tequila-Lime Sauce. Allow diners to assemble their own fajitas.

LAMB BROCHETTES WITH CHIMICHURRI SAUCE

Serves: 3–4

1–1½ lbs. boneless lamb
1 recipe Chimichurri Sauce (page 176)

Cut lamb into uniform pieces—about 1½-inch cubes—and thread onto skewers. Grill over hot flame until medium rare (130–135°), 8 to 10 minutes. Serve immediately with Chimichurri Sauce. Good over rice, or on tortillas.

CARNITAS

Serves: 6

3 lb. boneless pork butt
4 cloves garlic, minced
½ teaspoon oregano
1 bay leaf
½ cup dry white wine
1 teaspoon freshly ground black pepper
¾ teaspoon salt
½ cup water
tortillas, warmed
guacamole
chopped tomatoes
sour cream or *crema* (optional)

Cut pork into 1-inch cubes and place in large heavy pot along with garlic, oregano, bay leaf, wine, pepper, and salt. Bring to boil over medium heat. Stir, then partially cover and cook at a bare minimum simmer for 2 hours.

Remove cover and add ½ cup water. Increase the heat to medium-high and continue cooking, stirring every 10 minutes or so, until the pork is very soft and shreds easily when prodded, about 1 hour.

Remove and discard the bay leaf. Remove pork to serving dish with a slotted spoon and pull the pork into shreds with two forks.

Spread about ⅓ cup of meat in the center of a warmed tortilla. Top with guacamole, chopped tomatoes, and (if desired) sour cream or *crema*. Fold and serve. (I let everyone assemble their own tortillas to individual tastes.)

Note: Ashore, I make this in a crockpot using ¾ cup wine, and omitting the ½ cup water. Left to cook all day, it makes a heavenly aroma to come home to! This is the best way to make carnitas. On the boat, I cook carnitas in a pressure cooker at high pressure for 40 minutes.

TENACATITA PORK TENDERLOIN

This succulent and delicious tenderloin was the centerpiece of a delightful progressive dinner one Christmas in Tenacatita.

Serves: 10

2 pork tenderloins (about 2 ½ lbs.)
½ cup Dijon mustard
2 cloves garlic, minced
¼ cup dry red wine
¼ cup olive oil
1 tablespoon thyme
1 bay leaf
¼ teaspoon coarsely ground black pepper
½ teaspoon sugar

Trim fat from the tenderloins. Rinse, pat dry, and set aside in a glass pan or heavy duty Ziploc bag. Combine all other ingredients in a bowl. Pour marinade over the tenderloins, turn the tenderloins to coat with marinade, and cover the pan or seal the bag. Refrigerate for 6 hours or overnight.

Bring tenderloins to room temperature (about 30 minutes). Preheat oven to 400°. Line the bottom of a roasting pan with aluminum foil and place tenderloins on the foil. Roast until an instant read thermometer registers 140°, about 20–25 minutes. Frequently, different parts of the tenderloin reach 140° at different times, so use your best judgment. Do not overcook. Remove from oven and slice.

CHILE VERDE BURRITOS

Serves: 2–3

½ cup onion, chopped
2 teaspoons canola oil
¾ lb. pork tenderloin, cubed
1 clove garlic, minced
½ teaspoon salt
1 teaspoon cumin
3 tomatillos, finely chopped
1—4-oz. can diced green chiles, drained
1 tomato, finely chopped
1½ tablespoons sugar
½ cup chicken broth
6 flour tortillas, warmed
sour cream or *crema*
salsa

Heat oil in a large skillet. Add onion, pork, and garlic, and cook until onion is soft. Add salt, cumin, tomatillos, chiles, tomato, sugar, and chicken broth, and simmer 20 minutes. Additional chicken stock may be added if necessary for desired consistency.

Spoon chili verde onto flour tortillas, roll up, tucking the ends in. Serve with sour cream and salsa.

BASIC QUESADILLAS

Quesadillas are the grilled cheese sandwich of Mexico. They are generally a cheap and reliable item on restaurant menus, and quesadillas are great for a quick meal aboard.

flour tortillas
sliced or grated cheese, *Asadero*, *Chihuahua*, or Monterey jack
additions as desired: diced green chiles, chopped cooked bacon, diced ham, etc.

Cover half of each tortilla with cheese and any other desired additions. Fold tortilla to cover the cheese. Cook in skillet (preferably nonstick) over medium-high heat until tortilla is lightly browned. Turn and cook on other side until tortilla is lightly browned and cheese is melted. Continue until all quesadillas are cooked. Cut into wedges and serve with salsa, guacamole, *crema*, or bottled hot pepper sauce.

STACKED QUESADILLAS WITH CHORIZO AND GOAT CHEESE

These quesadillas are very rich and quite spicy. Serve them as a first course, or to accompany a soup or salad as a main course.

Serves 3–4 (or 6–8 as an appetizer)

8 oz. chorizo
6—6-inch flour tortillas
½ cup crumbled goat cheese
½ cup grated Monterey Jack
salt and pepper
Tomatillo Salsa (page 175)

Preheat oven to 450°. Remove chorizo from its casing and cook in a skillet over medium-high heat until browned.

Place 2 tortillas on an ungreased baking sheet. Cover each with ¼ of the cheeses and ¼ of the cooked chorizo and season with salt and pepper. Top each with another tortilla. Cover that tortilla with the remaining cheese and chorizo. Top each stack with a third tortilla. The quesadillas may be prepared to this point up to 4 hours ahead and refrigerated.

Bake quesadillas for 8–12 minutes, or until the tortillas are slightly crisp and the cheese is melted. Cut each quesadilla into quarters and serve hot, with Tomatillo Salsa.

CHILORIO AND EGGS

We make this easy dish whenever we want something quick and filling—breakfast, lunch, or dinner. Frequently we will whip up a batch when arriving in an anchorage at the end of a passage or a long day trip.

Serves: 2 generously

1—170-gram can *chilorio* (seasoned pork)
5 eggs
warmed flour or corn tortillas
sour cream or *crema*

Heat nonstick skillet over medium heat. Add *chilorio* and break up with a fork. Cook until *chilorio* is lightly browned, about 5 minutes. Reduce heat to low. Beat eggs with a fork, then add to the *chilorio*. Cook, stirring constantly, until the eggs are just set. Remove from heat and serve with tortillas and *crema*.

SPAGHETTI CARBONARA

Serves: 4

8–12 oz. spaghetti
4 slices ham, chopped
1 shallot, minced
1 cup chicken broth
½ cup frozen peas
½ cup sour cream or *crema*
1 pinch ground nutmeg
salt and pepper to taste
¼ cup shredded parmesan cheese

Cook the spaghetti until just tender, drain well.

While the spaghetti is cooking, sauté the ham and shallots in a large nonstick skillet over medium heat for 1 minute, or until the shallots begin to soften and the ham begins to brown. Add the broth and cook for 3 minutes, or until the liquid is reduced by half. Stir in the peas and heat through. Stir in the sour cream and continue cooking until the sauce is thick enough to coat the back of a spoon. Add the spaghetti and toss with the nutmeg, add salt and pepper to taste. Serve sprinkled with the parmesan cheese.

JENNIFER'S ANGEL HAIR WITH KALAMATA OLIVES

My friend, Jennifer, showed me how to make this dish using ingredients that I generally have in my galley. This recipe is perfect for impromptu suppers or unexpected guests, since it's as quick as it is delicious. The saltiness of the cheese really complements a nice red wine.

Serves: 2

angel hair pasta
about ½ jar Kalamata olive spread or tapenade
2 tablespoons butter
freshly grated Romano or Parmesan cheese

Bring pot of water to boil. Cook pasta for 2 minutes. Drain quickly and return to pot. Add olive spread, grated cheese, and butter. Toss and serve.

The quantities of the various ingredients vary with your individual taste. Add enough olive spread that the pasta is well-flecked with olives. Roughly a tablespoon of butter per person is about right. Add LOTS of cheese - and put additional cheese on the table for individual toppings.

STRAW AND HAY

Serves: 4

nonstick cooking spray
1 clove garlic, minced
1 small onion, diced
4 oz. mushrooms, sliced
1 cup frozen peas
4 oz. ham, chopped
¼ teaspoon basil
1 pinch ground nutmeg
8 oz. fettuccine, mixed white and green, if possible
1 small can evaporated milk
¼ teaspoon pepper
¼ teaspoon salt
¼ cup grated parmesan cheese

Spray a large skillet with cooking spray. Add garlic and onion and cook slowly until soft. Add mushrooms and sauté quickly.

Add peas and ham and heat through. Season with basil and nutmeg.

Meanwhile cook green and white fettuccine according to package directions. Do not overcook. Drain, add to the skillet, and toss all together.

Add evaporated milk, salt, pepper, and cheese. Heat through and serve.

Note: This recipe can be easily modified for camping, remote cabins, or boats without refrigeration. Substitute canned mushrooms, peas, and ham for times when refrigeration is not available.

FRIED RICE

Serves: 3–4 hungry people

3½ cups boiled or steamed rice, cold
3 eggs, lightly beaten
3 tablespoons scallion, minced
2 cloves garlic, minced
3 tablespoons canola oil
1 cup frozen peas
1 cup cooked ham, beef, pork, chicken, shrimp, or bacon, diced
½ cup shredded carrots (optional)
1 tablespoon soy sauce
1 tablespoon sesame oil (see Substitutions chapter)
salt and pepper to taste

Combine eggs with the scallion, scramble over medium-low heat until set, and set aside. Brown garlic in oil in a large nonstick skillet. Add the peas, meat and carrots (if using). Cook briefly, then add soy sauce.

Remove half of the meat mixture from the skillet and place in a bowl. Mix the cold rice with sesame oil and salt. Add ½ of the rice mixture to the meat mixture in the skillet and stir-fry until rice is hot and lightly browned. Add ½ of the scrambled eggs and mix.

Remove fried rice from the skillet to a serving bowl or platter. Add remaining meat mixture to the skillet and heat through. Add the remaining rice and stir-fry until done. Mix in the remaining scrambled eggs, remove to serving bowl or platter. Serve immediately, garnished with additional minced scallions, if desired.

PIZZA

½ recipe Basic Pizza Dough (page 151)
olive oil
toppings: tomato sauce, cheese, pepperoni, olives, etc.

Preheat oven to 475°. Roll out dough to fit on oiled cookie sheet. Brush top of crust with olive oil. Cover with desired toppings, and bake for 10–15 minutes, until cheese is melted and crust is lightly browned. Remove from oven and brush crust with olive oil.

Some possible combinations:
Tomato sauce, mozzarella or *Oaxaca* cheese, salami, sliced olives, diced bell pepper
Smoked salmon and brie
Goat cheese, sun-dried tomatoes, and roasted garlic
Fresh mozzarella, fresh tomatoes, and fresh basil
Parmesan cheese, tomato slices, avocado slices, rings of red onion, fresh basil

BLACK BEANS AND RICE

Serves: 4

1 onion, chopped
1 red pepper, chopped
1 tablespoon olive oil
2 cloves garlic, minced
1—14 oz. can black beans, drained
½ cup rice
1 ½ cups chicken broth
¼ teaspoon red pepper flakes
¼ teaspoon thyme
1 bay leaf
shredded cheese

Saute onion and red pepper in oil. Add garlic, black beans, rice, chicken broth, red pepper flakes, thyme, and bay leaf. Bring to a boil, then simmer 20 minutes. Remove bay leaf and serve, topped with shredded cheese.

VEGETARIAN SUPPER DISH

Serves: 4

½ cup chopped onion
2 cloves garlic, minced
1 medium zucchini, chopped
1 green pepper, chopped
½ teaspoon oregano
2 tomatoes, chopped
1—14-oz. can kidney beans, drained
shredded cheese

Saute onion and garlic. Add zucchini, green pepper, and oregano and cook until veggies are crisp-tender, about 5 minutes. Add tomatoes and kidney beans. Cover and heat thoroughly. Serve immediately over hot rice, sprinkled with shredded cheese.

Soups, Salads, and Side Dish Recipes

GAZPACHO

Serves: 10

3 medium, ripe beefsteak tomatoes
3 red bell peppers
2 small cucumbers
½ sweet white onion, minced
2 cloves garlic, minced
2 teaspoons salt
⅓ cup sherry vinegar (substitute white or red wine vinegar)
ground black pepper
5 cups tomato juice
1 teaspoon hot pepper sauce (optional)
8 ice cubes (if available)
extra-virgin olive oil (for serving)
Garnishes: finely diced avocado, red bell pepper, and cucumber

Process tomatoes in food processor for twelve 1-second pulses; transfer to a large bowl. Process peppers and cucumbers, separately, for about twelve 1-second pulses each. Add to bowl with tomatoes. Add the onion, garlic, salt, vinegar, and ground pepper to taste. Let stand until vegetables begin to release their juices, about 5 minutes. Stir in tomato juice, hot pepper sauce, if using, and ice cubes; cover tightly and refrigerate to blend flavors, at least 4 hours and up to 2 days.

Adjust seasonings with salt and pepper, remove and discard any unmelted ice cubes, and serve cold. Drizzle each portion with about 1 teaspoon high-quality olive oil and garnish with finely diced avocado, red bell pepper, and cucumber.

Note: We frequently make a half recipe of gazpacho, although leftover soup will keep for a couple of days.

COLD AVOCADO SOUP

Serves: 2 as main course; 4 as appetizer

1 can chicken broth, chilled
2 large, ripe avocados
juice of 1 lime
½ cup cream, milk, or buttermilk
½ cup sour cream, *crema*, or plain yogurt
½ teaspoon hot pepper sauce
salt and pepper to taste
optional garnishes: sour cream, chopped chives, chopped tomatoes, *picante* sauce

Chill the chicken broth. Cut the avocados in half, remove the pits, and scoop the pulp into a food processor or blender. Add the lime juice and cream. Blend until smooth.

Pour the avocado mixture into a bowl or storage container. Add the sour cream, chicken broth, hot pepper sauce, and salt and pepper. Serve immediately, or store in the refrigerator tightly covered until serving.

Garnish with one or more of the following garnishes: a dollop of sour cream, a sprinkling of chopped chives or tomatoes, or a drizzle of *picante* sauce.

SWEET POTATO-PEANUT BUTTER SOUP

Serves: 4

1—14 oz. can chicken broth
1 cup water
1 large onion, chopped
2 stalks celery, chopped
1 clove garlic, minced
2 medium sweet potatoes, chopped
1 bay leaf
¼ teaspoon thyme
¼ teaspoon Tabasco sauce
3 tablespoons peanut butter, preferably smooth style
2 teaspoons rice vinegar
¼ cup dry-roasted peanuts, chopped
¼ cup green onions, chopped

In large saucepan, combine chicken broth, water, onion, celery, garlic, sweet potatoes, bay leaf, thyme, and Tabasco and bring to boil over moderate heat. Simmer gently, covered, for 20–25 minutes or until potatoes are tender. Remove from the heat, discard the bay leaf, and stir in the peanut butter and vinegar.

Whirl vegetable mixture in food processor until pureed. Serve hot or chilled, garnished with peanuts and/or green onions.

CARROT AND LEEK SOUP

Serves: 4

½ lb. leeks
2 cloves garlic, crushed
1 tablespoon butter
1 lb. carrots, trimmed and cut into 2-inch pieces
½ lb. red potatoes, peeled and quartered
2 cups chicken broth
¼ cup fresh dill, chopped
¼ teaspoon ground black pepper
1 cup water

Trim the leeks, split them lengthwise and wash them carefully under cold running water to remove any grit and sand. Cut the leeks into 2-inch pieces.

Place the leeks, garlic and butter in a medium saucepan, cover and cook over low heat 5 minutes. Add the carrots, potatoes, broth, dill, pepper, and 1 cup of water, increase the heat to medium-high and bring mixture to a boil. Cover the pan, reduce the heat to low and simmer the soup 15–20 minutes, or until the potatoes are tender.

Remove the pan from the heat, uncover it and allow the soup to cool 20 minutes.

Transfer the soup to a food processor or blender and process until smooth, then return it to the pan and reheat 5–10 minutes over medium heat. Ladle the soup into 4 bowls and serve.

LEEK AND POTATO SOUP

4 cups leeks, cleaned thoroughly and sliced
4 cups potatoes, diced
6 cups water
1½ teaspoons salt

Bring the leeks, potatoes, and water to a boil in a heavy bottomed saucepan. Salt lightly, cover partially, and simmer 20–30 minutes, or until the vegetables are tender. Taste, and correct seasoning.

Ladle out soup and top each serving with a dollop of sour cream or *crema*, if you wish.

Variation #1: Puree the soup and whisk ⅔ cup sour cream, *crema*, or heavy cream into the soup.

Variation #2, Spinach Soup: Chop 20 ounces of fresh spinach. Add to the Leek and Potato Soup and simmer 4–5 minutes, then puree. Top with sour cream or *crema*.

CALDO DE QUESO

This soup is an interesting change of pace for lunch or a light supper. The taste is mildly spicy with a flavor that is cheesy, but not overwhelmingly so. The soup is quite similar to the broth served in *molcajetes*, the lava cauldrons served full of boiling broth, vegetables, and meat or seafood at restaurants on the mainland coast.

Serves: 4

4 tablespoons olive oil
½ cup chopped onion
2 jalapeños, seeded and minced
2 potatoes, peeled and diced
2 tomatoes, chopped
2 sprigs cilantro, minced
3 cups chicken broth
2 cups milk
8 oz. panela or Chihuahua cheese, diced
salt and pepper to taste

Heat 2 tablespoons olive oil in a skillet. Add onion and jalapenos; sauté until onion starts to wilt. Remove from heat and set aside.

In a saucepan, heat the remaining 2 tablespoons of olive oil; sauté potatoes until almost cooked. Add tomatoes and simmer 10 minutes. Add onion-jalapeno mixture, cilantro, and chicken broth; bring to a boil. Reduce heat and add milk; simmer 20 minutes. Add cheese; season with salt and pepper, and serve immediately.

CACTUS SALAD

In large Mexican grocery stores, you may see a booth in the produce department with a lady pulling spines from *nopales* (prickly pear cactus paddles). You can buy the paddles whole, split, or diced.

Serves: 4

2 cups *nopalitos* (diced tender cactus)
2 medium tomatoes, coarsely diced
½ medium white onion, minced
1 serrano or jalapeño, minced
3 tablespoons vegetable oil
1 tablespoon cider vinegar
2 tablespoons chopped cilantro
2 tablespoons crumbled *queso fresco*, *panela*, or feta cheese

Rinse and drain the cactus. Place cactus pieces in a medium bowl. Add the tomatoes, onion, chiles, oil, vinegar, and cilantro. Mix well. Serve the salad topped with crumbled cheese.

BANANA, APPLE, AND PEANUT SALAD

Serves: 4

¼ cup honey
½ teaspoon grated lemon or lime zest
3 tablespoons lemon or lime juice
½ teaspoon salt
¼ teaspoon ground ginger
⅛ teaspoon nutmeg
1 lb. bananas, peeled and sliced into ½-inch pieces
1 lb. apples, diced into ½-inch pieces
⅔ cup dry roasted peanuts, chopped

In large bowl, whisk together the honey, lemon zest, lemon juice, salt, ginger, and nutmeg. Add bananas, apples and peanuts. Toss and serve.

WALDORF SALAD

Serves: 4–6

1 cup diced apples
1 tablespoon lime or lemon juice
1 cup diced celery
½ cup grapes, halved and seeded (optional)
½ cup chopped walnuts (optional)
½ to ¾ cup mayonnaise

In a medium bowl, toss the apples with lime or lemon juice. Add the celery, grapes, and nuts and toss again. Stir in mayonnaise and serve at room temperature or cold.

CRUNCHY CABBAGE SALAD

Just about everyone loves this salad. Good for potlucks and great for cruising.

Serves: 8

½ cup slivered almonds
1 tablespoon sesame seeds
½ head green cabbage, shredded
4 green onions, chopped
1 pkg. chicken-flavored ramen noodles
2 teaspoons sugar
3 tablespoons cider vinegar
3 tablespoons canola oil

Toast almonds and sesame seeds. Toss with chopped cabbage and green onions. Crunch up the dry Ramen noodles and add to the cabbage mixture.

Combine sugar, vinegar, oil, and the seasoning packet from the Ramen noodles. Just before serving, add dressing to cabbage mixture and toss ingredients well.

RED CABBAGE SLAW

Serves: 4

½ head red cabbage, shredded
1 red bell pepper, seeded and sliced thin
½ cup fresh basil leaves, shredded
2 tablespoons balsamic vinegar
1 teaspoon honey
½ teaspoon salt
¼ teaspoon pepper
2 tablespoons olive oil

Combine cabbage, pepper, and basil in large bowl. Whisk vinegar, honey, salt, and pepper together in small bowl until honey has dissolved. Whisk in oil, pour dressing over cabbage, and toss well.

PERFECT PICNIC POTATO SALAD

Serves: 4–6

2 lb. potatoes (preferably russet), peeled and cut in ¾-inch dice
1 tablespoon salt

Dressing:
2 tablespoons white vinegar
½ cup finely chopped celery
2 tablespoons minced red onion
3 tablespoons sweet pickle relish
½ cup mayonnaise
¾ teaspoon dry mustard
¾ teaspoon celery seed
2 tablespoons minced fresh parsley
¼ teaspoon ground black pepper
½ teaspoon salt
2 large eggs, hard-boiled and cut into ¼-inch cubes (optional)

Place potatoes in large saucepan and add water to cover by 1 inch. Bring to boil over medium-high heat. Add 1 tablespoon salt, reduce heat to medium and simmer until potatoes are tender, about 8 minutes.

Drain potatoes and transfer to large bowl. Add vinegar and toss gently, using rubber spatula, to combine. Let stand until potatoes are just warm, about 20 minutes.

In small bowl, combine celery, onion, pickle relish, mayonnaise, dry mustard, celery seed, parsley, pepper, and ½ teaspoon salt. Using rubber spatula, gently fold the dressing into the potatoes, along with the eggs, if using. Cover and refrigerate until chilled.

GERMAN POTATO SALAD

Serves: 6–8

2 lb. small red potatoes, scrubbed and halved
1 tablespoon salt
8 oz. bacon, cut crosswise into ½-inch pieces
1 medium onion, finely chopped
½ teaspoon sugar
½ cup white vinegar
½ cup reserved cooking water
1 tablespoon hearty mustard
¼ teaspoon ground black pepper
¼ cup minced fresh parsley

Place potatoes, salt, and water to cover in large saucepan. Bring to boil over high heat, then reduce heat to medium and simmer until potatoes are tender, about 10 minutes. Reserve ½ cup of the cooking water, then drain potatoes. Return potatoes to the pan and cover to keep warm.

While potatoes are cooking, fry the bacon in a large skillet over medium heat, stirring occasionally, until brown and crisp, about 5 minutes. Transfer bacon to paper towel-lined plate using a slotted spoon. Pour off all but ¼ cup of bacon grease. Add onion to the skillet and cook over medium heat until softened and beginning to brown, about 4 minutes. Stir in sugar until dissolved. Add vinegar and reserved cooking water. Bring to simmer and cook until mixture is reduced to about 1 cup, about 3 minutes. Remove from heat and whisk in mustard and pepper. Add potatoes, parsley, and bacon to skillet and toss to combine. Serve warm.

MAZATLAN POTLUCK SALAD

Serves: 8–10

1—15 oz. can yellow corn, drained
1—15 oz. can white corn, drained (substitute: another can of yellow corn)
1—15 oz. can black beans, drained
1 medium cucumber, seeded and diced
1 medium green bell pepper, seeded and diced
2 plum tomatoes, diced
4 green onions, sliced
2 tablespoons minced parsley
1 clove garlic, minced

Dressing:
⅓ cup olive oil
2 tablespoons red wine vinegar
1 teaspoon sugar
¼ teaspoon dry mustard
¼ teaspoon curry powder
salt and pepper to taste

Combine the corn, beans, cucumber, green pepper, tomatoes, green onions, parsley, and garlic in a large bowl. In a small bowl or jar, whisk or shake together the dressing ingredients. Toss with the vegetables. Refrigerate, covered, for 4 hours for the flavors to blend.

TOMATO AND CUCUMBER SALAD

Serves: 4

5 small tomatoes
1 medium cucumber
1 small red onion

Dressing:
1 tablespoon Greek seasoning mix
1 tablespoon water
¼ cup olive oil
½ cup red wine vinegar
½ teaspoon salt
¼ teaspoon freshly ground pepper

Mix Greek seasoning with water and let stand for 5 minutes. Wash the tomatoes and cut into wedges. Wash the cucumber, cut off the ends, and score the edges with a fork. Cut into ¼-inch slices or half slices. Peel onion, cut into rings, then cut rings in half.

Whisk the remaining dressing ingredients into the Greek seasoning and water until well blended. Put the veggies into a bowl and toss with dressing. Let stand awhile to marinate.

GREEN BEAN SALAD

Serves: 6

Blanched Green Beans, chilled (see page 139)
2 strips lime or lemon peel, minced
1 clove garlic, minced
¼ teaspoon salt
1½ tablespoons Dijon mustard
1½ tablespoons lime or lemon juice
½ cup olive oil
additional salt and pepper to taste

Mash the minced lemon or lime peel, minced garlic, and ¼ teaspoon of salt into a paste. Beat in the mustard and 1 tablespoon of lime or lemon juice. When thoroughly blended, beat in the oil by droplets to make a homogeneous sauce. Beat in more lemon or lime juice, salt, and pepper to taste.

Toss chilled green beans with the dressing. You may add slivered red bell peppers for color, if desired.

JICAMA SALAD

Serves: 6

1 medium jicama, peeled
1 small carrot, peeled and shredded
¼ cup orange juice
1 tablespoon lime juice
1 teaspoon rice vinegar (substitute: white wine vinegar)
1 tablespoon olive oil
1 tablespoon chopped cilantro or parsley
¼ teaspoon salt

Cut jicama into julienne strips, about 2 inches long and ¼-inch wide. Put into a medium bowl. Add carrot shreds and toss. Combine remaining ingredients in a jar and shake. Pour dressing over the salad and toss. Serve cold.

BLACK BEAN AND JICAMA SALAD

Serves: 4

1 can black beans, drained and rinsed
1 cup jicama, peeled and finely diced
1 cup *panela* or feta cheese, crumbled
3 tablespoons lime juice
¼ cup minced cilantro
2 sliced green onions
2 teaspoons honey
¼ teaspoon crushed red pepper flakes

In a bowl, combine beans, jicama, cheese, lime juice, cilantro, onions, honey, and red pepper flakes. Mix well. If made ahead, cover and refrigerate for up to 4 hours.

MONTA'S SPINACH SALAD

Serves: 4

1 bag washed spinach
½ large red onion, halved and sliced thin
1 small can mandarin oranges, drained
½ cup diced dates or blueberries
½ cup pine nuts, pecans, or other nuts, toasted
Poppyseed Dressing (recipe follows)

Toss all ingredients in a large bowl with Poppyseed Dressing. Serve immediately.

Poppyseed Dressing

2 tablespoons sugar
½ teaspoon salt
½ teaspoon dry mustard
3 tablespoons white wine vinegar
½ cup olive or canola oil
½ tablespoon poppy seeds

Place dressing ingredients in a covered jar and shake well. Dress salad just before serving. Store remaining dressing in refrigerator.

MEXICAN RICE

Serves: 4

1 small carrot, peeled and cut into ¼-inch dice
1 tablespoon vegetable oil
1 cup white rice
½ medium onion, chopped
2 garlic cloves, minced
¼ teaspoon cumin
½ cup canned pureed tomatoes (*pure de tomate*)
1 cup chicken broth
½ cup water
¼ teaspoon salt
¼ teaspoon pepper

In a small saucepan of boiling salted water, cook carrot until just tender, about 3 minutes. Drain and rinse under cold running water; drain well.

In a large saucepan, heat oil over medium heat. Add rice and cook, stirring, about 1 minute to coat with oil. Stir in onion and garlic. Cook, stirring, until onion is translucent, about 3 minutes.

Stir in cumin, tomato puree, chicken broth, water, salt, and pepper. Bring to a boil. Reduce heat to low, cover, and cook 15–18 minutes, or until liquid is absorbed and rice is tender. Remove from heat and let stand 5 minutes. Add cooked carrot and stir gently to combine. Serve hot.

ROASTED POTATOES WITH SMOKED PAPRIKA

Until 2005, I had never cooked with smoked paprika. After I discovered this recipe, smoked paprika became a staple on Legacy. It provides a wonderful, complex flavor to many recipes.

Serves: 4

1½ lb. baby potatoes (or new potatoes, quartered)
2 tablespoons olive oil
1 teaspoon salt
1 tablespoon smoked paprika

Preheat oven to 350°. Toss the potatoes and olive oil in a roasting pan. Season with salt and paprika and toss again. Roast until potatoes are soft, about 40 minutes, stirring now and then.

EASY SCALLOPED POTATOES

Serves: 4–6

2 tablespoons butter
1 medium onion, finely chopped
2 cloves garlic, minced
1 teaspoon thyme
1¼ teaspoons salt
¼ teaspoon pepper
2½ lbs potatoes, peeled and sliced ⅛-inch thick
1 cup chicken broth
1 cup heavy cream
2 bay leaves
1 cup (4 oz.) shredded Cheddar or *Chihuahua* cheese

Preheat oven to 425°. Melt butter in large Dutch oven over medium-high heat until foaming subsides. Add onion and cook, stirring occasionally, until soft and lightly browned, about 4 minutes. Add garlic, thyme, salt, and pepper; cook until fragrant, about 30 seconds. Add potatoes, chicken broth, cream, and bay leaves and bring to simmer. Cover, reduce heat to medium-low, and simmer until potatoes are almost tender (paring knife can be slipped into and out of potato slice with some resistance), about 10 minutes. Discard bay leaves.

Transfer mixture to 8-inch square baking dish; sprinkle evenly with cheese. Bake until cream is bubbling around the edges and top is golden brown, about 15 minutes. Cool 10 minutes before serving.

OVEN FRIED POTATOES

This recipe is great when you need a fix of French fries!

Serves: 4

3 russet potatoes, peeled and sliced lengthwise into 10 wedges
5 tablespoons vegetable or peanut oil
¾ teaspoon salt
¼ teaspoon pepper

Preheat oven to 475°. Place potato wedges in large bowl and cover with hot water; soak 10 minutes. Meanwhile, coat a large heavy-duty rimmed baking sheet (or 2 smaller sheets) with 4 tablespoons oil and sprinkle evenly with ¾ teaspoon salt and ¼ teaspoon pepper; set aside.

Drain potatoes. Spread potatoes out on triple layer of paper towels and thoroughly pat dry with additional paper towels. Rinse and wipe out now empty bowl; return potatoes to bowl and toss with remaining 1 tablespoon of oil. Arrange potatoes in single layer on prepared baking sheet; cover tightly with foil and bake 5 minutes. Remove foil and continue to bake until bottoms of potatoes are spotty golden brown, 15–20 minutes, rotating baking sheet after 10 minutes. Using metal spatula and tongs, scrape to loosen potatoes from pan, then flip each wedge, keeping potatoes in single layer. Continue baking until fries are golden and crisp, 5–15 minutes longer, rotating pan as needed if fries are browning unevenly.

Transfer fries to paper towels to drain. Season with additional salt and pepper to taste and serve hot.

ORANGE AND RUM SWEET POTATOES

Serves: 4

1 teaspoon canola oil
3 medium sweet potatoes, peeled and diced
¾ cup chicken broth
½ cup orange juice
1 tablespoon rum
2 teaspoons honey
2 teaspoons cornstarch
salt and pepper to taste
1 tablespoon minced parsley

Heat oil in a large nonstick skillet over medium-high heat. Add potatoes and ½ cup of broth. Bring to boil, then reduce heat, cover, and simmer until potatoes are tender when pierced (about 10 minutes). Uncover and continue to cook, stirring occasionally, until liquid has evaporated and potatoes are tinged with brown (about 5 more minutes).

In a bowl, mix remaining ¼ cup broth, orange juice, rum, honey, and cornstarch. Add cornstarch mixture to pan and bring to boil over medium heat. Cook, stirring, just until thickened. Season to taste with salt and pepper, and sprinkle with parsley.

CUMIN-SCENTED CARROTS

Serves: 6

2 tablespoons butter
1 tablespoon olive oil
6 medium carrots, peeled and sliced on a angle into oval rounds ¼-inch thick
½ teaspoon ground cumin
½ teaspoon salt
⅛ teaspoon pepper
1 tablespoon minced cilantro or parsley

In a large skillet, melt butter with olive oil over medium-high heat. Add the carrots and cook, tossing frequently, 3–4 minutes. Stir in the cumin, salt, and pepper. Reduce heat to low, cover, and cook until carrots are tender but still firm, 2–3 minutes. Garnish with cilantro or parsley and serve.

ROASTED PEPPER MÉLANGE

Serves: 6

2 large red peppers
2 large green peppers
2 large yellow peppers
2 tablespoons white wine vinegar
2 cloves garlic, minced
½ teaspoon salt
¼ teaspoon black pepper
1 tablespoon olive oil
2 tablespoons minced fresh basil
2 tablespoons minced parsley
1 tablespoon capers, drained and chopped (optional)

Preheat the broiler, setting rack 6 inches from the heat. Line a broiler pan with aluminum foil and arrange the whole bell peppers on their sides on the pan. Broil the peppers, turning frequently, for 10–12 minutes or until they are charred on all sides. Gently lift the aluminum foil off the broiler pan and wrap it around the peppers. (Note: you can also roast the peppers on the grill, then place in a paper bag to cool.) Place on a cutting board and let stand for 5 minutes.

Using a thin knife, scrape the skin off the peppers and discard. Remove the core, seeds, and ribs, cut the peppers lengthwise into 1-inch wide strips and rinse them under cold water to remove the black bits. Arrange the strips on a platter. In a small bowl, whisk together the vinegar, garlic, salt, black pepper, and oil. Pour the dressing over the peppers and top with the basil, parsley, and, if desired, the capers. Serve warm, or at room temperature.

Sautéed Variation: Core and seed the peppers, and cut lengthwise into ½-inch strips. Omit the vinegar and garlic. Chop 1 medium-size yellow onion. In a large skillet, heat the oil over moderate heat. Add the onion and sauté for 3 minutes or until slightly softened. Add the peppers and sauté, stirring, for 5 minutes or until lightly browned and tender, but still slightly crisp. Stir in the salt, pepper, and herbs, and cook 1 minute more. Serve hot.

Note: This is an easy and elegant side dish for dinner parties; just about everyone who tastes this asks for the recipe!

BLANCHED GREEN BEANS

Serves: 6

1½ lb. fresh green beans

Wash and drain the beans. Snap off the ends and pull down to remove strings. French the beans by slicing into 1½-inch to 2-inch slanting strips about ³⁄₁₆-inch wide.

Bring a large pot of salted water to a rapid boil (1½ teaspoons of salt per quart of water). Drop the prepared beans into the boiling water. Cover briefly to bring the water quickly back to a boil, then immediately remove the cover. Boil uncovered until the beans are just cooked through but still slightly crunchy (2–3 minutes).

Immediately when the beans are done, dump them into a colander and drain off all the water. If not serving at once, quickly chill with cold water and ice (if available). When chilled, wrap the beans in a clean dry towel and refrigerate in a plastic bag.

To reheat: Just before serving, turn the beans into a large nonstick skillet and toss over moderately high heat for a moment to evaporate excess moisture. Then toss with salt, pepper, and softened butter.

Note: Blanching and quickly cooling the beans results in a lovely bright green color and nice crunch. Great used cold in Green Bean Salad [page 131].

ROASTED GREEN BEANS

Serves: 4

1 lb. green beans, stem ends snapped off
1 tablespoon olive oil
½ teaspoon salt
freshly ground pepper

Preheat oven to 450°. Line baking sheet with aluminum foil; spread beans on baking sheet. Drizzle with oil and toss to coat evenly. Sprinkle with ½ teaspoon salt, toss to coat, and distribute in even layer. Roast 10 minutes.

Remove baking sheet from oven. Using tongs, redistribute the beans. Continue roasting until beans are dark golden brown in spots and have started to shrivel, 10–12 minutes more.

Adjust seasoning with salt and pepper, and serve.

Variation: Roasted Green Beans with Red Onion and Walnuts

1 tablespoon balsamic vinegar
1 teaspoon honey
½ teaspoon thyme
2 cloves garlic, sliced thinly
½ medium red onion, cut into ½-inch thick wedges
1 lb. green beans, stem ends snapped off
salt and pepper to taste
⅓ cup walnuts, toasted and chopped

Combine balsamic vinegar, honey, thyme, and garlic, and set aside. Roast red onion along with the beans, as in the original recipe. When you remove the beans and onion from the oven after the initial roasting period, combine them with vinegar/honey mixture. Continue roasting. When done, season to taste with salt and pepper, transfer to serving dish, and top with walnuts.

SAUTÉED *CALABACITAS*

Serves: 4

1½ lbs. *calabacitas* or other small summer squash
3 tablespoons olive oil
3 tablespoons minced fresh parsley
2 cloves garlic, minced
1 teaspoon grated lime or lemon zest (optional)
salt and pepper to taste

Dice or slice squash into ½-inch thick pieces. Heat oil in large skillet over high heat. Drop in squash a handful at a time and let each gain a little color before adding the next handful. Sauté until all the squash is golden and tender, about 7 minutes.

Remove squash to a serving bowl and toss with parsley, garlic, grated lime or lemon zest (optional), and salt and pepper to taste.

Note: A great way to fix any of the summer squashes found in Mexico. Vary the recipe by tossing the cooked squash with different seasonings.

ASPARAGUS WITH WARM LEMON DRESSING

Serves: 4

1 lb. asparagus
1 medium shallot, peeled and crushed
1 clove garlic, peeled and crushed
2 teaspoons olive oil
2 tablespoons white wine
1 tablespoon lemon or lime juice
¼ teaspoon freshly ground black pepper

Wash the asparagus, then snap off and discard the tough bottoms. Steam the asparagus until tender.

Meanwhile, sauté the shallot and garlic in the olive oil. Add wine and cook over low heat until the alcohol evaporates and the garlic turns golden, about 10 minutes. Discard the garlic and shallot. Whisk the lemon juice and pepper into the oil and wine, pour over the steamed asparagus, and serve.

ZUCCHINI SKILLET

Serves: 3–4

3 medium potatoes
1 large onion, preferably red
½ cup olive oil
2 zucchini or 4 *calabacitas*
salt and pepper

Cut potatoes and onion into ¼-inch dice. Place ¼ cup olive oil in each of 2 large skillets (or cook in two batches) and heat over medium-high burner. When oil is hot, add ½ the potato mixture to each skillet and toss to coat with oil. Cook 6 minutes.

Cut zucchini into ½-inch dice. Add ½ the zucchini to each skillet and toss. Cook about 14 minutes until the veggies are tender and golden brown. Season to taste with salt and pepper.

Bread and Breakfast Recipes

Cruisers frequently find baking difficult in the propane oven on their boat. There are a couple of secrets to getting good results. First, invest in a simple oven thermometer so you can tell what the temperature actually is in the oven. Second, make sure to preheat the oven. Third, unlock the gimbals on your stove and remove any heavy pans from the stovetop to ensure even rising. To avoid burning, rotate the baking pan one or more times to ensure even browning, check the temperature periodically throughout the baking process, and turn down the oven midway, if needed. And on the inevitable occasions when something does burn, just trim off the worst and serve it anyway!

BASIC WHITE BREAD

Although I don't make bread very often aboard Legacy, every cruiser should have a good basic bread recipe available. If you make this reliable recipe a few times, you'll soon learn the feel of well-kneaded bread dough.

Makes: 1 large loaf or 2 smaller loaves

1 tablespoon active dry yeast
1¼ cups warm (105–115°) water
2 teaspoons sugar
3¾ cups flour
1 tablespoon salt

Proof the yeast by dissolving in ½ cup of the warm water, adding the sugar, stirring well, and letting sit for a few minutes. While yeast is proofing, measure 3¾ cups unsifted flour in a large bowl. Add salt and blend well. Pour about ¾ cup of the warm water into flour and stir with wooden spoon. Add yeast mixture and continue stirring until dough forms a ball.

Transfer dough to lightly floured surface and knead, adding flour as necessary, until dough has a smooth, satiny, elastic feeling (5–10 minutes). Let dough rest for several minutes, then place in buttered bowl. Roll dough around until coated with butter, then cover bowl with plastic wrap and set in warm place. Let rise until doubled, about 1–2 hours.

Punch down the dough, knead again for about 3 minutes, then pat into smooth oval. Let rest for 4–5 minutes, then form into loaf. Place in large, buttered loaf pan (or 2 smaller pans) and let rise again—about 45 minutes. Meanwhile preheat oven to 450°.

Bake for 10 minutes at 450°, then reduce temperature to 350°. Bake for another 30 minutes or so until the loaf sounds hollow when rapped on the bottom. Remove the loaf from the pan and allow to cool on a rack or clean dish towel.

HOMEMADE FLOUR TORTILLAS

Makes: 12 tortillas

2 cups white flour
1 teaspoon salt
5 tablespoons lard (substitute: vegetable shortening)
½ cup warm water
more lard
more flour

Put the flour and salt into a mixing bowl and mix them together until blended. Add the 5 tablespoons lard to the bowl and mix the lard into the flour mixture with your hands until the lard is evenly distributed. The texture should be something like cornmeal. Add the water to make a soft, easily kneaded dough. Turn the dough out and knead it for about three minutes (don't over knead). The dough should have a nice velvety texture.

Divide the dough into 12 equal pieces. Roll each piece into a ball and coat with a little melted lard. Place all the balls in a bowl and cover with a moist towel. Let the dough rest at least 15 minutes, and as long as two hours.

Flatten the dough balls with the heel of your hand on a lightly floured surface and roll into thin tortillas about 5–6 inches in diameter. (If the dough feels rubbery and resists rolling try letting it rest a while longer, also add a little more water to the dough next time.) I find that rolling once in one direction and then flipping and turning the tortilla and rolling once in the other direction several times gives a nice round shape.

Cook the tortillas one at a time in a heavy pan preheated over medium heat. As soon as small bubbles form, flip the tortilla and cook the other side until very lightly browned. The tortillas should cook quickly. Tortillas will keep for several days in the refrigerator.

CREAM BISCUITS

Serves: 4

2 cups flour
2 teaspoons sugar
2 teaspoons baking powder
1½ teaspoons salt
1½ cups heavy cream (*crema para batir*)

Preheat oven to 425°. Line baking sheet with parchment paper, if available.

Whisk together flour, sugar, baking powder, and salt in medium bowl. Add 1¼ cups cream and stir with wooden spoon until dough forms, about 30 seconds. Transfer dough from bowl to countertop, leaving all dry, floury bits behind in the bowl. In 1-tablespoon increments, add up to ¼ cup cream to dry bits in bowl, mixing after each addition, until moistened. Add these moistened bits to rest of dough and knead by hand just until smooth, about 30 seconds. The dough should be quite soft and a bit sticky. If it is too dry and stiff, knead in a bit more cream.

Shape the dough into a round, ¾-inch thick. Cut into rounds with a biscuit cutter or cut into wedges with knife. Place rounds or wedges on baking sheet and bake until golden brown, about 15 minutes, rotating baking sheet halfway through baking.

Note: These biscuits are both easy and wonderfully decadent! Good with jam or Isabelle's Lemon Butter (recipe follows).

Isabelle's Lemon Butter

My Scottish grandmother, Isabelle, was never known as a cook, but her Lemon Butter (or lemon curd) was a family treat when I was growing up. It wasn't until I was an adult and made her recipe for the first time that I learned how easy it is. Isabelle's Lemon Butter is also wonderful over gingerbread.

Makes: about 1 pint

¼ lb. butter
2 cups sugar
¾ cup lemon juice (substitute: lime juice)
3 large eggs, beaten

To sterilize a pint jar, fill it with boiling water, cover with the lid, and let it sit for at least five minutes. Melt butter and sugar together in top of double boiler (I use a metal mixing bowl that just fits into the top of a medium saucepan). Add lemon juice (¾ cup takes 3–6 lemons) and beaten eggs. Cook gently until it thickens to about the consistency of heavy cream. Pour into sterilized jar and refrigerate.

HEATHER'S ENGLISH MUFFINS

Makes: 12 muffins.

1 tablespoon active dry yeast
2 tablespoons 105–115° water
1 cup water
½ cup milk
2 teaspoons sugar
1 teaspoon salt
4 cups all-purpose flour
3 tablespoons butter, softened

Dissolve yeast in 2 tablespoons of warm water. Combine 1 cup water, milk, sugar, salt, and yeast mixture. Gradually beat in 2 cups flour. Cover loosely with plastic wrap. Let rise in warm area for 2 hours or until dough collapses back into the bowl.

Beat in butter. Beat or knead in remaining flour. Press dough to a thickness of ½ inch and cut out with muffin rings, biscuit cutter, or a glass. If not using muffin rings, wrap a narrow strip of plastic wrap around the edge of each muffin and place them side by side in a lightly greased 9 x 13 inch pan. Let the muffins stand until dough has doubled in bulk. Carefully slip a thin pancake turner under the muffin, remove plastic wrap or muffin rings, and transfer to a medium-hot, well-buttered griddle or skillet. Cook until light brown on the first side, turn and cook until light brown on the other side, about 8 minutes total. Cool on rack. Split muffins with a fork before toasting. Serve with butter, peanut butter, or jam.

HONEY YOGURT SCONES

Serves: 6

4 tablespoons butter
1 tablespoon honey
½ cup plain yogurt
1 large egg
1¾ cups flour
½ teaspoon baking powder
½ teaspoon baking soda
¼ teaspoon salt
¼ cup dried currants, dried cherries, chopped dried apricots, pecans, or raisins

Preheat oven to 400°. Melt together butter and honey in small bowl. Remove from heat and whisk in yogurt and egg.

In a medium mixing bowl, sift together flour, baking powder, baking soda, and salt. Stir in dried fruit and/or nuts. Pour egg mixture over flour mixture and, using a fork, very gently cut together just until dough is beginning to come together but is not quite completely combined.

Turn out onto a lightly floured surface and gently pat into a 6-inch circle. Fold dough in half and pat out again. Repeat 2–3 more times, taking care not to over-work the dough. Pat into a 1-inch thick circle (about 6 inches in diameter) and cut into six wedges.

Place on an ungreased baking pan. Brush lightly with beaten egg (optional) and bake for 12–15 minutes, until puffed and golden brown. Remove from oven and serve immediately with lots of butter and jam.

Note: Especially nice made with a mélange of lightly toasted nuts. Toast walnuts, cashews, hazelnuts, and macadamia nuts in a dry pan before including in the scones.

BANANA BREAD

Serves: 8

1⅓ cups flour
¾ teaspoon salt
½ teaspoon baking soda
¼ teaspoon baking powder
5⅓ tablespoons butter
⅔ cup sugar
2 large eggs, lightly beaten
1 cup mashed very ripe bananas (about 2 bananas)
½ cup coarsely chopped walnuts or pecans

Preheat oven to 350°. Grease a 8½ x 4½ inch loaf pan. Whisk together flour, salt, baking soda, and baking powder. In a large bowl, beat the butter and sugar on high speed until lightened in color and texture, 2–3 minutes. Beat in the flour mixture until blended. Gradually beat in the eggs. Fold in the banana and nuts until just combined.

Scrape the batter into the loaf pan and spread evenly. Bake until a toothpick inserted in the center comes out clean, 50–60 minutes. Let cool in pan for 5–10 minutes, then remove from pan and cool completely before slicing.

LIME NUT BREAD

Makes: 1 loaf

1 cup sugar
½ cup butter, softened
3 eggs
2½ cups flour
2 teaspoons baking powder
1 teaspoon salt
⅔ cup milk
2 tablespoons lime juice
1 tablespoon grated lime zest
¾ cup chopped pecans or walnuts

Glaze:

1 cup powdered sugar, sifted
4 teaspoons lime juice

Beat together sugar and butter in large bowl. Add eggs, one at a time, beating after each addition. Combine flour, baking powder, and salt. Add to butter mixture alternately with milk. Beat in lime juice and zest; stir in nuts. Pour into greased loaf pan. Bake at 350° for 50–60 minutes or until toothpick inserted near center comes out clean. Cool in pan for 10 minutes. Remove from pan and continue cooling on wire rack.

Meanwhile make lime glaze by combining sugar and lime juice. Mix well. Drizzle over loaf and slice thinly to serve.

FRESH LIME OR LEMON MUFFINS

Serves: 8

1¾ cups flour
½ cup sugar
1½ teaspoons baking powder
½ teaspoon baking soda
¼ teaspoon salt
grated zest of 2 limes or lemons
½ cup melted butter
⅔ cup fresh lime or lemon juice
2 teaspoons lemon extract (optional)
2 large eggs

Glaze:

¼ cup sugar
¼ cup fresh lime or lemon juice

Preheat oven to 400°. In a large bowl, combine flour, sugar, baking powder, baking soda, salt, and zest. In another bowl, mix butter, lime juice, extract and eggs. Stir wet mixture into dry ingredients just until moistened. Spoon into greased muffin cups, mounding full.

Bake for 20–25 minutes, or until lightly browned around edges and springy to touch. Meanwhile, make lime glaze: combine sugar and lime juice in a small saucepan. Heat to just dissolve sugar. Do not boil. Set aside. Pierce baked muffins in a few places. Pour warm lemon glaze over the muffins. Cool in pan 5 minutes to absorb glaze before removing to cool completely on a rack.

NORMA'S FEATHERLIGHT ROLLS

Makes: 20 rolls

1 tablespoon dry yeast
¼ cup lukewarm water
¼ cup shortening
¾ cup scalded milk
¼ cup sugar
1 teaspoon salt
1 large egg
3½ cups flour

Dissolve yeast in water. Melt shortening in scalded milk and add sugar, salt, and egg. When mixture has cooled to lukewarm, add the dissolved yeast. Stir in flour and knead 5–10 minutes, until dough is smooth, adding up to ¼ cup additional flour if needed. Let rise until doubled in bulk (45–60 minutes). Form into 20 rolls and place 10 in each of two greased loaf pans. Let rise until light (about 45 minutes). Bake at 375° for 10–15 minutes or until done.

BASIC PIZZA DOUGH

Makes: 2 crusts

1 tablespoon sugar
1 cup warm (105–115°) water
1 tablespoon active dry yeast
3½ cups flour
1 teaspoon salt
¼ cup olive oil

Dissolve the sugar in 1 cup warm water. Dissolve the yeast in the sugar water and proof. Combine 3 cups flour, salt, the yeast mixture, and oil in medium bowl. Beat well until mixed, adding more water or flour if necessary. Knead about 5 minutes.

Let rise until double, about 1 hour. Punch down and shape into two balls. Use immediately or wrap in plastic wrap and freeze. Makes two crusts. When ready to use, proceed as instructed in the recipe for Pizza (page 120).

PERFECT OATMEAL

This recipe makes a wonderful, hearty, nutty-flavored bowl of oatmeal that is delicious served with chopped nuts and dried fruit, honey, butter, milk, or cream. It is possible to substitute regular rolled oats, but not quick-cook oatmeal.

Serves: 2–3

3 cups water
1 cup whole milk
1 tablespoon butter
1 cup steel-cut oats
¼ teaspoon salt

Bring water and milk to simmer in large saucepan over medium heat. Meanwhile, heat butter in medium skillet over medium heat until just beginning to foam; add oats and toast, stirring constantly with wooden spoon, until golden and fragrant with butterscotch-like aroma, 1½–2 minutes.

Stir toasted oats into the simmering liquid, reduce heat to medium-low; simmer gently, until mixture thickens and resembles gravy, about 20 minutes. Add salt and stir lightly with wooden spoon handle. Continue simmering, stirring occasionally with spoon handle, until oats absorb almost all liquid and oatmeal is thick and creamy, with a pudding-like consistency, about 7–10 minutes. Off heat, let oatmeal stand uncovered 5 minutes. Serve immediately.

BREAKFAST EGG BAKE

This is an easy breakfast recipe to serve a crowd. On Legacy, we've served it to crew on overnight races. I prepare all the ingredients in advance, then assemble and bake in the morning.

Serves: 8

12 slices white bread, crust removed
nonstick cooking spray
4 oz. ham, diced
2 cups milk
8 eggs
¼ cup minced onions
½ teaspoon dry mustard powder
¼ teaspoon paprika
¼ teaspoon salt
2 oz. shredded Cheddar or *Chihuahua,* or *Asadera* cheese
1 tablespoon dried parsley

Preheat oven to 400°. Cut bread into cubes and spread over bottom of a 7 x 11 inch or 9 x 13 inch pan that has been sprayed with cooking spray or lightly oiled. Sprinkle ham on top of bread.

Using a mixer or blender, combine milk, eggs, onion, mustard, paprika, and salt. Pour over ham. Sprinkle with shredded cheddar and parsley. Bake for 35–40 minutes, or refrigerate overnight and bake in the morning.

HUEVOS RANCHERO

Serves: 4

¼ cup canola oil
1 medium onion, finely chopped
2 large tomatoes, finely chopped
1 serrano pepper, minced
1 tablespoon minced cilantro
½ teaspoon salt
⅛ teaspoon pepper
4 corn tortillas
4 eggs
¼ cup crumbled feta or *queso fresco*
2 cups refried beans

In a medium saucepan, heat 2 tablespoons oil over medium heat. Add onion and cook 3–5 minutes. Add tomatoes, serrano pepper, cilantro, ¼ teaspoon. salt, and pepper. Bring to a boil, reduce heat, cover, and simmer for 10 minutes. Sauce can be prepared in advance and reheated.

While sauce cooks, heat remaining 2 tablespoons oil in a large nonstick skillet over medium heat. Add tortillas, one at a time, and cook about 20 seconds on each side. Drain on paper towels.

In same skillet, bring the sauce to a gentle simmer. Remove from heat and make four shallow wells in the sauce with the back of a large spoon. Break 1 egg into a cup and pour into the well. Repeat with other three eggs. Season each egg with salt and pepper, cover skillet, and place over medium-low heat. Cook until desired doneness: 4–5 minutes for runny yolks, 6–7 minutes for set yolks.

Place tortillas on serving plates. Gently scoop one egg onto each tortilla. Spoon sauce around each egg, covering tortillas but leaving part of the eggs exposed. Sprinkle crumbled cheese on top. Add hot refried beans to each plate and serve.

Dessert Recipes

Cruisers always appreciate desserts at potlucks or for a special treat aboard. Don't be afraid to bake aboard. Check out the tips at the beginning of Bread and Breakfast Recipes and fire up that oven to make a birthday cake, a Thanksgiving pie, or cookies for Superbowl Sunday!

BANANA NUT QUESADILLA

Serves: 4

2 large bananas or 6 tiny bananas (*platano domingo*)
4 flour tortillas
½ cup cream cheese
2 tablespoons honey-roasted nuts, chopped
¼ cup caramel sauce

Peel the bananas and slice lengthwise about ¼-inch thick. If you are using large bananas, cut the slices crosswise so they are 3–4 inches long. Lay out the tortillas and spread 2 tablespoons of the cream cheese over the entire surface of each tortilla. Top half of each tortilla with banana slices and sprinkle with ½ tablespoon of the nuts. Fold the tortillas in half.

Heat a large nonstick skillet over medium heat until hot. Place 2 of the tortillas in the pan and cook until golden brown, about 2 minutes per side. Repeat for the remaining tortillas.

Cut each tortilla into 3 wedges and drizzle with 1 tablespoon of the caramel sauce.

Note: Caramel sauce (*cajeta*) is popular and widely available in Mexico. Leftover sauce is good on saltine crackers as a snack.

PINEAPPLE RICE PUDDING

Serves: 8

2 cups water
1 cup rice
2 cinnamon sticks
3 cups milk
¾ cup sugar
¼ teaspoon salt
3 egg yolks
1 teaspoon vanilla
1—8 oz. can crushed unsweetened pineapple
½ cup sliced almonds, toasted

In a medium saucepan, bring 2 cups of water to a boil over high heat. Add rice and cinnamon sticks. Reduce heat to low, cover, and simmer until rice is tender and liquid is absorbed, about 18–20 minutes.

Stir in milk, sugar, and salt. Continue cooking over medium-low heat. Simmer uncovered, stirring frequently, until thickened and creamy, about 15–20 minutes. Remove cinnamon sticks.

Beat egg yolks and vanilla together in a small bowl until blended. Beat 3 tablespoons of hot rice pudding into the yolks. Then quickly stir the yolk mixture into the hot rice pudding, mixing well. Cook, stirring, over low heat for about 2 minutes. Stir in drained pineapple and transfer to serving bowl. Top with toasted almonds. May be served warm or cold.

GRILLED BANANAS WITH RUM SAUCE

4 large unpeeled bananas
⅔ cup light brown sugar, packed (substitute: grated *piloncillo*)
¼ cup lime juice
¼ cup dark rum
⅛ teaspoon allspice
⅛ teaspoon nutmeg

On BBQ or stovetop grill pan, grill the unpeeled bananas 10–11 minutes, turning occasionally, until blackened. When cool enough to handle, slit the banana skins with a paring knife and carefully peel off. Cut the bananas on the diagonal into ½-inch slices.

Meanwhile, in a medium saucepan, combine the brown sugar, lime juice, and rum. Bring to a gentle boil over medium heat. Stir in the allspice and nutmeg. Add the sliced bananas, and cook until piping hot and well coated, about 3 minutes. Spoon the bananas onto 4 plates and serve.

CREMA DE MANGO

This creamy dessert can be eaten like mousse, or used as a topping for cakes, ice cream, or other fruits.

Serves: 6

2 large ripe mangoes
1 teaspoon lime juice
1 cup heavy cream (*crema para batir*)
1 tablespoon sugar
½ tablespoon vanilla extract
½ cup toasted pecan (or other nut) bits

Peel mangoes and cut fruit away from the pit. Puree with the lime juice in a food processor.

In a medium bowl, whip the cream until thickened. Add the sugar and vanilla, and beat until stiff. Fold the mango puree into the whipped cream. Serve at once or refrigerate for up to 2 hours. Garnish with pecans or other nuts.

CHOCOLATE BROWNIES

Makes: 16

3 oz. unsweetened chocolate
1 stick butter
1 cup sugar
1 teaspoon baking powder
¼ teaspoon salt
2 large eggs
1 teaspoon vanilla
⅔ cup flour

Preheat oven to 350°. Line 8-inch square pan with foil and coat foil with cooking spray or oil. Melt chocolate and butter in small bowl, stirring occasionally. Cool mixture for several minutes.

Whisk together sugar, baking powder, salt, eggs, and vanilla until combined, about 15 seconds. Whisk in chocolate mixture until smooth. Stir in flour until no streaks of flour remain. Scrape batter evenly into prepared pan.

Bake until toothpick inserted halfway between edge and center of pan comes out clean, 22–27 minutes. Cool brownies on wire rack about 2 hours. Using foil, lift brownies from pan to cutting board. Slide foil out, then cut brownies into 2-inch squares.

COCOA BROWNIES

This recipe for brownies uses only cocoa, so you can get a chocolate fix even if you are miles from the nearest chocolate bar or bag of chocolate chips.

Makes: 36 brownies

1 cup (2 sticks) butter or margarine
2 cups sugar
2 teaspoons vanilla extract
4 eggs
¾ cup cocoa
1 cup all-purpose flour
½ teaspoon baking powder
¼ teaspoon salt
1 cup chopped nuts (optional)

Preheat oven to 350°. Grease a 9 × 13 inch baking pan.

Melt the butter and place in mixing bowl. Stir in sugar and vanilla. Add eggs, one at a time, beating well with spoon after each addition. Add cocoa; beat until well blended. Add flour, baking powder and salt; beat well. Stir in nuts, if desired. Pour batter into prepared pan.

Bake 30–35 minutes or until brownies begin to pull away from sides of pan. Cool completely in pan on wire rack. Frost if desired. Cut into bars.

PEANUT BUTTER COOKIES

I made these cookies for a SuperBowl Party in Tenacatita and turned them into football cookies. First, I rolled the dough into small balls as called for in the recipe. As I put them on the cookie sheets, I stretched them into ovals with pointed ends. Then, using a table knife, I drew a lengthwise line for the seam of the ball before pressing them flat with a fork to make the lacing.

Makes: 60 cookies

½ cup unsalted butter
½ cup sugar
½ cup packed brown sugar (substitute: grated *piloncillo*)
1 large egg
1 cup peanut butter
½ teaspoon salt
½ teaspoon baking soda
½ teaspoon vanilla
1 to 1½ cups flour

Preheat the oven to 375° and grease cookie sheets. Beat the butter until soft. Add the sugars gradually and blend until creamy. Beat in the egg, peanut butter, salt, baking soda, and vanilla. Mix in the flour, using the larger amount if your peanut butter is heavy in oil.

Roll the dough into small balls. Place on a greased cookie sheet and press flat with a fork. Bake 10–12 minutes.

RITA'S PEANUT BUTTER BARS

These bars, made by Rita on Overheated, are always a popular dish at Mayor's Night Out dinghy raft-ups in Tenacatita. For our tastes, I use the lower amounts of sugar.

Makes 24 bars

Crust:
½ cup butter (1 stick), softened
½ cup peanut butter
1¼–1½ cups sugar
½ teaspoon vanilla
1½ cups flour

Filling:
2 eggs
2 tablespoons peanut butter
⅓–½ cup sugar
⅓–½ cup packed brown sugar

Preheat oven to 375°. For crust, mix in a medium bowl butter, peanut butter, and sugar until well blended. Stir in vanilla. Add flour and mix well. Mixture will be crumbly. Reserve about 1 cup of the crust mixture for topping. Firmly press remaining mixture into the bottom of a lightly greased 9 × 13 inch pan.

For filling beat together eggs, peanut butter, and the two sugars. Spread over the unbaked crust. Sprinkle with reserved crust mixture. Bake for about 20 minutes, or until set and top is golden. Cool in pan and cut into bars.

CREAM CHEESE ICEBOX COOKIES

Icebox cookies are a boon onboard. The frozen or chilled dough is easier to handle in hot climates than most cookie dough. In addition, if you have a log of cookie dough lurking in your freezer, it's easy to produce hot, fresh cookies on short notice for guests or a potluck.

Makes about 42 cookies

2 cups flour
½ teaspoon salt
½ teaspoon baking powder
⅛ teaspoon baking soda
11 tablespoons butter, softened
1 cup sugar
1 large egg
3 oz. cream cheese, softened and cut into chunks
1 teaspoon vanilla
¼ teaspoon finely grated lime or lemon zest (optional)
cinnamon and sugar mixture (optional)

Whisk together flour, salt, baking powder, and baking soda. Beat the butter, sugar, and egg on medium speed until fluffy and well-blended. Gradually beat in the cream cheese, vanilla, and zest (if using). Stir the flour mixture into the butter mixture until smooth. Refrigerate until slightly firm, about 1 hour. Scrape the dough onto a large piece of plastic wrap or wax paper. Using the plastic wrap and a rubber spatula, form the dough into a log about 12–14 inches long. Roll the log completely in plastic wrap and freeze at least three hours (preferably) or refrigerate for several hours. The log of dough can be sealed in a plastic bag and frozen for up to a month.

When ready to bake cookies, preheat oven to 375° and grease cookie sheets. Remove the dough from the freezer or refrigerator and slice crosswise into ⅛-inch thick slices. Place slices on greased cookie sheets, about 2 inches apart. Sprinkle with cinnamon sugar, colored sugar, or other decorations, and bake until cookies are tinged with brown at the edges, 7–11 minutes. Let stand on sheet until the cookies firm slightly, then transfer to a rack or clean dish towel to cool.

HI-TEST ICEBOX COOKIES

Makes about 50 cookies

4 teaspoons Kahlua
2 teaspoons instant expresso powder (substitute: instant coffee)
½ lb. butter, softened
¾ cup packed dark brown sugar
¼ teaspoon cinnamon
⅛ teaspoon salt
2½ cups flour

Stir together Kahlua and instant expresso or coffee in a small bowl. Beat butter and sugar on medium speed until well-blended and smooth. Add expresso mixture, cinnamon, and salt, and beat until blended. Gradually add the flour, ½ cup at a time, beating on low speed after each addition. Scrape the dough onto a large piece of plastic wrap or wax paper. Using the plastic wrap and a rubber spatula, form the dough into a log about 12–14 inches long. Roll the log completely in plastic wrap and freeze at least three hours or refrigerate for several hours. The log of dough can be sealed in a plastic bag and frozen for up to a month.

When ready to bake cookies, preheat oven to 350° and line cookie sheets with parchment paper or greased aluminum foil. Remove the dough from the freezer or refrigerator, then slice crosswise into ¼-inch thick slices. If frozen, allow the dough to thaw slightly before slicing. Place slices on greased cookie sheets, about 1 inch apart. Bake until tops look dry and slightly brown around the edges, about 12 minutes. Let stand on sheet until the cookies firm slightly, then transfer to a rack or clean dish towel to cool.

FIVE-MINUTE FUDGE

2 tablespoons butter
⅔ cup evaporated milk (1 small can)
1⅔ cups sugar
½ teaspoon salt
2 cups miniature marshmallows
8 oz. semisweet chocolate chips (substitute: 1½—150 gram bars *semiamargo* baking chocolate, chopped into pieces)
1 teaspoon vanilla
½ cup chopped walnuts or pecans

Put butter, evaporated milk, sugar, and salt in heavy saucepan over medium heat and bring to a boil. Cook 4–5 minutes, stirring constantly. Start timing when mixture starts to bubble around the edges. Remove from heat.

Stir in miniature marshmallows, chocolate chips, vanilla, and nuts. Stir vigorously for 1 minute (until marshmallows melt and blend) and pour into buttered 8-inch square pan. Cool, and cut into squares.

FAST AND EASY PEANUT BUTTER FUDGE

2 cups sugar
½ cup water
1 cup peanut butter (smooth or chunky)
1 teaspoon vanilla extract
3 tablespoons cocoa (optional)

Butter an 8-inch square pan. Place peanut butter and vanilla in a bowl and set aside. Mix sugar, water, and optional cocoa (if using) in a saucepan, and bring to a boil. Boil rapidly for exactly one minute. Pour over the peanut butter and vanilla, and beat until thick. Pour into the buttered pan and allow to cool. Cut into squares.

FLAKY PIE CRUST

Makes: 2–9-inch crusts

2½ cups flour
1 teaspoon sugar
1 teaspoon salt
1 cup vegetable shortening or lard, or ½ cup each shortening and butter
⅓ cup plus 1 tablespoon cold water

Using a rubber spatula, combine flour, sugar, and salt in a large bowl. Add shortening or shortening/butter mix and break the shortening into large chunks. Using a pastry blender, cut the fat into the dry ingredients. If you don't have a pastry blender, use 2 knives, one held in each hand, and cut in opposite directions. As you work, occasionally stir dry flour up from the bottom of the bowl. Continue until some of the fat remains in pea-sized pieces and the remainder is the consistency of coarse crumbs or cornmeal.

Drizzle over the flour mixture ⅓ cup plus 1 tablespoon cold water. Using the rubber spatula, cut with the blade side until the mixture looks evenly moistened and begins to form small balls. Press down on the dough with the flat side of the spatula. If the balls of dough stick together, you have added enough water. If not, add an additional 1–2 tablespoons of cold water and again cut it in. The dough should look rough not smooth, so don't overwork it.

Divide the dough in half, press each half into a flat disk, and wrap tightly in plastic. Refrigerate for at least 1 hour or for up to 2 days before rolling. The dough can also be tightly wrapped and frozen. Thaw completely before rolling.

CRUMB PIE CRUST

Makes: 1–9-inch crust

Graham crackers, vanilla wafers, gingersnaps, or similar cookies
6 tablespoons melted butter
¼ cup sugar
¼ teaspoon cinnamon (optional)

Preheat oven to 350°. Using food processor, process crackers or cookies into fine crumbs. Alternatively, put the cookies in a plastic Ziploc bag and crush with rolling pin. You will need 1½ cups of crumbs.

Mix all ingredients with a fork or pulse in a food processor until all ingredients are moistened. Spread mixture evenly in pie pan, using fingertips to press the mixture over the bottom and up the sides of the pan. Bake until crust is lightly browned and firm to touch, about 10–15 minutes. Allow to cool before filling.

AHWAHNEE'S KEY LIME PIE

Kathy on Ahwahnee made this pie, which was a hit at the Christmas progressive dinner in Tenacatita. It uses ingredients readily available in Mexico and avoids the use of raw eggs "cooked" by the lime juice, which is common in key lime pie recipes. Ready-made graham cracker crusts are available at Sam's Club and some large supermarkets. Otherwise, there are many lightly sweetened Mexican cookies that would make good crust. We like using Polvorones, which are an orange-flavored cookie.

Serves: 6

1—8 oz. package cream cheese
1—15 oz. can sweetened condensed milk (397 gram can *La Lechera*)
⅓ cup lime juice (takes about 5 medium limes)
1 teaspoon grated lime zest
1 teaspoon vanilla
green food coloring (optional)
1 graham cracker crust
whipped cream for topping

Blend cream cheese and sweetened condensed milk. Add lime juice, grated zest, vanilla, and the optional food coloring, if using. Pour into graham cracker crust and refrigerate until set. Shortly before serving, add whipped cream topping if desired.

CHOCOLATE-WALNUT PIE

Serves: 8

3 oz. semisweet baking chocolate (*semiamargo*)
3 tablespoons butter
4 large eggs
½ cup sugar
1 cup light corn syrup
2 cups walnuts, large pieces or halves
3 tablespoons Kahlua
1–9-inch unbaked pie crust

Heat oven to 350°. In top of double boiler over hot, not boiling, water, melt chocolate and butter. Remove from heat and set aside to cool completely.

In a medium bowl, with a fork beat the eggs with sugar and corn syrup until light and fluffy. Blend in chocolate. Stir in nuts and Kahlua.

Pour into pie shell and bake 40 minutes or until center is set. Note that a toothpick will NOT come out clean when inserted in center; pie will firm up as it cools. Let stand at least 1 hour at room temperature before serving. Can be made 3–4 days in advance. Cover with plastic wrap and refrigerate.

PUMPKIN PIE

Serves: 6–8

1—15 oz. can pumpkin (or 2 cups cooked pumpkin)
1—12 oz. can evaporated milk
¾ cup sugar (all white, or mixture of white and brown)
½ teaspoon salt
1 teaspoon cinnamon
½ teaspoon ginger
½ teaspoon nutmeg or allspice
¼ teaspoon cloves
2 large eggs
1 unbaked 9-inch pie crust

Preheat oven to 425°. Beat eggs in a large bowl. Beat in pumpkin, sugar, salt, cinnamon, ginger, nutmeg, and cloves. Gradually stir in evaporated milk.

Pour pumpkin mixture into prepared pie crust. Bake at 425° for 15 minutes. Reduce heat to 350°. Bake for an additional 40–50 minutes until knife inserted near center comes out clean. Cool for 2 hours before serving.

CARROT CAKE (*PASTEL ZANAHORIA*)

1 lb. (6–7 medium) carrots, peeled
4 large eggs
1½ cups sugar
½ cup packed light brown sugar (substitute: grated *piloncillo*)
1½ cups canola oil
1¼ teaspoons baking powder
1 teaspoon baking soda
1¼ teaspoons cinnamon
½ teaspoon nutmeg
⅛ teaspoon cloves
½ teaspoon salt
2½ cups flour
1 recipe Cream Cheese Frosting

Preheat oven to 350°. Butter or oil a 9 × 13 inch baking pan. Shred the carrots coarsely. Beat the eggs and the sugars together in a large bowl until frothy. Add oil in a steady stream while beating the egg mixture. Stir in carrots.

Beat in the baking powder, baking soda, cinnamon, nutmeg, cloves, and salt. Stir in the flour and mix until no streaks of flour remain.

Pour batter into prepared pan and bake until toothpick inserted into the center of the cake comes out clean, 35–40 minutes, rotating pan halfway through the baking period. Cool cake to room temperature in the pan before frosting with Cream Cheese Frosting.

Cream Cheese Frosting

8 oz. cream cheese, softened but still cool
5 tablespoons unsalted butter, softened but still cool
1 tablespoon sour cream or *crema*
½ teaspoon vanilla extract
1¼ cups powdered sugar

Beat the cream cheese, butter, sour cream, and vanilla in medium bowl until combined. Add powdered sugar and beat until smooth.

Note: When I didn't have powdered sugar, I successfully made this frosting with ¾ cup regular sugar. The texture wasn't quite as nice, but as the frosting stood the graininess gradually diminished.

TORTUGA'S LORETOFEST RUM CAKES

Marilyn on Tortuga bakes these wonderful rum cakes in chocolate, orange, and coconut variations, which are easy make-in-advance potluck desserts.

TRIPLE CHOCOLATE RUM CAKE

1 package chocolate cake mix
1 package instant chocolate pudding mix
¾ cup water
½ cup rum
½ cup oil
4 eggs
1 cup chocolate chips

Glaze:
4 tablespoons butter
2 tablespoons water
½ cup sugar
¼ cup rum

Preheat oven to 350°. Combine cake mix, pudding, water, rum, oil, and eggs together for 1 minute on slow speed and 2 minutes on high. Add chocolate chips. Scrape batter into a greased and floured 9 × 13 inch pan and bake for 35–40 minutes. Cool for 5 minutes, poke holes all over the cake with a fork, and pour glaze over the cake.

For glaze, mix butter, water, and sugar in a small saucepan and heat until butter is melted and sugar dissolved. Add the rum and pour over the cake. If desired, sprinkle chocolate jimmies over the cake for an additional jolt of chocolate!

ORANGE RUM CAKE

1 package yellow or white cake mix
1 package vanilla or lemon instant pudding mix
¾ cup fresh orange juice
8 tablespoons melted butter
½ cup rum
4 eggs
1 tablespoon orange zest

Glaze:
4 tablespoons butter
½ cup sugar
¼ cup orange juice
¼ cup rum

Topping:
Toasted sliced almonds

Mix, bake, and glaze cake following the directions for the Triple Chocolate Rum Cake. Sprinkle glazed cake with toasted sliced almonds.

COCONUT RUM CAKE

1 package white cake mix
1 package vanilla instant pudding
8 tablespoons melted butter
¾ cup coconut cream
½ cup rum
4 eggs

Glaze:
4 tablespoons butter
2 tablespoons water
½ cup sugar
¼ cup rum

Topping:
Toasted coconut

Mix, bake, and glaze cake following the Triple Chocolate Rum Cake directions. Sprinkle glazed cake with toasted coconut.

LIGHTNING CAKE

This simple "lightning fast" cake is delicious with or without the topping, and can also be topped with icing or used as a base for one of the dessert sauces following. It is almost as easy as making a cake from a mix.

Serves: 8

1 cup flour
1 tablespoon baking powder
¼ teaspoon salt
8 tablespoons butter
1 cup sugar
3 large eggs
1 teaspoon grated lime or lemon zest
2 tablespoons fresh lime or lemon juice

Topping (optional):

⅓ cup chopped or sliced almonds or other nuts
1 heaping tablespoon sugar

Preheat oven to 350°. Whisk together thoroughly the flour, baking powder, and salt. In a large bowl, beat the butter until creamy. Gradually add the sugar and beat until lightened in color and texture, 3–5 minutes. Beat in the eggs, one at a time. Beat in the lime or lemon zest and juice. Stir in the flour mixture until just smooth.

Scrape the batter into a greased and floured 8-inch round pan. If desired, sprinkle the top with a mixture of almonds or other nuts and sugar. Bake until a toothpick inserted in the center comes out clean, 30–35 minutes. Let cool in the pan for 10 minutes. Slide a thin knife around the cake to detach it from the pan, and invert to remove from the pan, if desired.

HOT LIME SAUCE

Makes: 1⅓ cups

⅔ cup sugar
¼ cup lime juice
grated zest of 1 lime
2 tablespoons water
3 large egg yolks
8 tablespoons unsalted butter, cut into pieces

Combine sugar, lime juice, zest, and water in a small, heavy saucepan. Whisk in egg yolks until thoroughly blended. Add butter and set over low heat. Bring to a simmer, stirring constantly but gently, and cook until thickened, about 1 minute. Serve immediately, or refrigerate for up to 3 days. Reheat over low heat or over hot water.

CHOCOLATE SAUCE

Quick and delicious, this chocolate sauce is good over plain cake as well as on those rare occasions when we have ice cream aboard.

Makes: 1 cup

½ cup light cream, or ¼ cup heavy cream and ¼ cup milk
1–2 tablespoons sugar
1 tablespoon butter
4 oz. semisweet or bittersweet chocolate, finely chopped
1 tablespoon vanilla, or 1 tablespoon dark rum or Cognac

Combine cream, sugar, and butter in a medium, heavy saucepan and bring to a rolling boil, stirring constantly. Remove the pan from the heat and immediately add the chocolate. Let stand for 1 minute, then whisk until smooth. Whisk in vanilla, rum, or Cognac. Serve warm or cold. Sauce can be thinned with water as needed. May be refrigerated for up to 2 weeks and reheated over low heat.

Note: If you have a small food processor, you can use it to chop the chocolate. Then complete the sauce by pouring the simmering cream mixture in a stream into the processor while running. After the chocolate is melted and mixed into the cream mixture, add the vanilla, rum, or Cognac.

FRESH MANGO SAUCE

Makes 1¼ cups

1 large soft, but not mushy, mango
2 tablespoons sugar
2 tablespoons water
1 tablespoon strained fresh lime or lemon juice

Peel the mango and cut the flesh away from the pit. Combine the mango in a blender or food processor with sugar, water, and lime or lemon juice. Puree until smooth. If sauce is too thick, thin with a bit more water. If not sweet enough, add a little more sugar. Serve immediately, or cover and refrigerate for up to 3 days. Excellent served over plain cake, ice cream, or banana or coconut desserts.

BANANA SAUCE

Makes about 3 cups

½ cup packed brown sugar
4 tablespoons butter
¾ cup fresh orange juice
2 tablespoons fresh lime or lemon juice
¼ cup dark rum or brandy
¼ teaspoon cinnamon
¼ teaspoon allspice
½ teaspoon vanilla
3 firm ripe bananas, peeled and cut in ¼-inch dice

In a medium saucepan, melt sugar and butter over medium heat, stirring. Add orange juice and lime or lemon juice. Bring to a boil, stirring.

Reduce heat to low. Stir in rum or brandy, cinnamon, allspice, and vanilla. Add bananas and stir gently to combine. Cook until heated through, about 1 minute. Serve warm over cake or ice cream.

Sauce and Condiment Recipes

Sauces and condiments add spice and variety to your menus. Don't stick just to the recommended combinations of a food with a sauce. Try your own variations and you may hit on a new favorite!

EASY *CREMA* SAUCES

Any of the easy *crema* sauces below are excellent with simple sautéed or grilled fish or chicken. You can use the same basic techniques to invent your own sauce with a different flavor addition. If any of these sauces get too thick or need a extra bit of flavor, you can add a tablespoon or two of lime juice, vermouth, or white wine.

Easy Almond Sauce:

Finely chop ⅓ cup almonds. Toast in small skillet over medium heat until fragrant and slightly brown. Add one can Nestle *Media Crema* and warm. Season to taste with salt, pepper, and ¼–½ teaspoon ground *chipotle* or cayenne pepper. Serve warm over chicken or fish.

Easy Garlic Sauce:

Heat 1 tablespoon butter in small skillet over medium heat. Add 2 cloves minced garlic and sauté, stirring frequently, until garlic is fragrant and lightly browned. Add one can of Nestle *Media Crema* and stir over low heat until bubbly and slightly thickened. Remove from heat and stir in 1 tablespoon lime juice and salt and pepper to taste. Serve warm over fish or poultry.

Easy Dijon Sauce:

Melt 1 tablespoon butter in small skillet. Add 1 clove minced garlic and sauté briefly, until garlic is fragrant and slightly browned. Add 1 can Nestle *Media Crema* and 2 tablespoons Dijon mustard. Simmer until sauce is slightly thickened. Season to taste with salt and pepper, and a few drops of lime juice.

Easy *Chipotle* Sauce:

Combine 1 can Nestle *Media Crema* and 1 teaspoon *chipotle* hot sauce in a small saucepan or skillet. Bring to a boil and simmer until thickened. Add 1–2 tablespoons vermouth or white wine and simmer until alcohol is burned off and sauce is the desired thickness. Season with salt and pepper, and serve immediately. If you don't have *chipotle* hot sauce, you could substitute dried ground *chipotle* peppers, or pureed canned *chipotles*.

Easy Banana Sauce:

Heat 1 tablespoon butter in small skillet. Dice one ripe, but firm, banana and sauté in butter for a couple of minutes. Add one can Nestle *Media Crema* and bring to a simmer. Cook for a few minutes until sauce thickens slightly. Season to taste with salt, pepper, and a few drops of lime juice, and serve over chicken or fish.

TEQUILA-LIME SAUCE

1 cup sour cream or *crema*
1 tablespoon tequila
1 tablespoon lime juice

Combine all ingredients in a small saucepan. Set over medium heat and whisk until just boiling. Simmer 1 minute to burn off the alcohol and thicken the sauce. Remove from heat and use immediately, or cover and refrigerate for up to 3 days. Reheat before serving. Especially good with Lamb Fajitas (page 113).

TOMATILLO SALSA

8 tomatillos, husked and washed
1 tablespoon finely diced red onion
½ tablespoon minced jalapeño
2 tablespoons lime juice
2 tablespoons minced cilantro
1 tablespoon olive oil
1 teaspoon honey
salt and pepper to taste

Finely chop the tomatillos. Combine in a bowl with remaining ingredients. Serve immediately or refrigerate, covered, for up to one day. Bring to room temperature before serving.

BLACK BEAN SALSA

2—15-oz. cans black beans, rinsed and drained
½ teaspoon cumin
¼ teaspoon oregano
2 medium tomatoes, seeded and chopped
½ medium onion, finely chopped
3 serrano or jalapeño peppers, minced
2 tablespoons rice vinegar (substitute: white wine vinegar)
2 tablespoons lime juice
½ teaspoon salt
¼ cup olive oil
2 tablespoons minced cilantro

Combine all ingredients in a bowl and stir to combine. Serve at once or refrigerate.

CHIMICHURRI SAUCE

We first encountered this sauce at a wonderful restaurant in Mazatlan that serves pit-roasted lamb. It is equally good with other roasted or grilled meats.

Makes about 1 ¼ cups

¼ cup red wine vinegar
1 small onion, chopped
⅓ cup chopped parsley or cilantro
4 cloves garlic, minced
3 jalapeños, minced
1 teaspoon oregano (optional)
½ cup olive oil
salt and pepper to taste

Combine vinegar, onion, parsley or cilantro, garlic, jalapeños, and oregano (if using) in bowl of food processor and whirl until chopped finely and well-combined. Transfer to a bowl and stir in oil, salt, and pepper. Refrigerate for at least 2–3 hours to allow flavors to meld.

CITRUS-ONION SALSA

The cool taste of the citrus fruit is wonderful on spicy tacos. The version made with grapefruit is less sweet than the recipe made with oranges.

Makes 1 cup

1 large orange or small grapefruit
¼ cup diced onion
1 tablespoon minced jalapeño or serrano chiles
1 tablespoon cilantro leaves
⅛ teaspoon ground cumin

Peel the citrus fruit and dice into ¼-inch pieces, removing any seeds. Combine all ingredients in a bowl. Serve immediately or refrigerate, covered, and use within one day.

MANGO SALSA

Mango salsa is especially good on grilled fish, as well as poultry or pork.

1 ripe, but firm, mango
1 minced jalapeño or serrano chile
¼ cup finely chopped onion
1 tablespoon coarsely chopped cilantro
2 tablespoons lime juice
¼ teaspoon salt

Peel the mango. Using a paring knife, slice down to the pit at ¼-inch intervals, both horizontally and vertically. Cut the squares of pulp away from the seed.

Mix the mango and remaining ingredients in a bowl. Serve immediately.

FRESH PINEAPPLE SALSA

1 medium ripe pineapple
½ large red bell pepper, finely diced
3–4 serrano or jalapeño peppers, minced
4 scallions, minced
2 tablespoons rice vinegar (substitute: white wine vinegar)
1 teaspoon sugar
⅛ teaspoon salt
3 tablespoons cilantro, minced

Cut off top and bottom of pineapple. Cut lengthwise into quarters and cut out the core. Cut off the skin and remove eyes before chopping the pineapple into ⅜-inch chunks.

Place pineapple chunks into a large bowl and adding remaining ingredients. Mix well. Serve at room temperature, or cover and refrigerate for up to 4 hours.

PELAGIC'S DIABLA SAUCE

This and the two following sauces are all excellent with boiled shrimp or other seafood.

1 cup catsup
½ stick butter
¼ cup white wine
⅛ cup chile sauce, hot sauce, or *salsa mexicana* to taste

Heat catsup, butter, and white wine in small sauce pan to simmer. Add chile sauce or hot sauce to taste, about ⅛ cup. Simmer for a few minutes to blend the flavors. Serve hot.

COCKTAIL SAUCE

½ cup catsup
½ cup chili sauce or *salsa mexicana*
¼ cup finely grated horseradish
hot pepper sauce to taste
lime juice to taste

Mix all ingredients together in a small bowl. Will keep, refrigerated, for about a week.

GARLIC BUTTER

2 cloves garlic, minced
1 stick butter

Melt 2 tablespoons butter in a small skillet. Add garlic and cook over low heat until just starting to brown. Add remaining butter, melt, then simmer over low heat for 3 minutes. Serve hot.

MEXICAN TARTAR SAUCE

1 cup mayonnaise
2 tablespoons chopped capers
1 tablespoon minced onion
1 serrano or jalapeño pepper, seeded and minced
1 tablespoon cilantro, minced
1 tablespoon lime juice

Combine all ingredients in a small bowl. Serve within 2–3 hours for best flavor. Excellent served with fish or shrimp.

PICKLED ONIONS

2 medium red or white onions
½ cup red wine vinegar
1 tablespoon sugar
3 tablespoons water

Halve onions and slice thinly. Place in a bowl. In a small nonreactive saucepan, combine remaining ingredients. Bring to a boil, and then pour over the onions. Set aside to marinate at least 15 minutes, or cover, refrigerate, and use within 2 weeks.

Wonderful with *arrachera* or grilled meats.

FRIED SQUASH BLOSSOMS

We knew that squash blossoms made great soup but when we found the whole fresh blossoms in the market, we had to try them. They have a pleasant mild taste, and the coating gives them a nice crunch.

½ cup milk, or 1 egg mixed with ¼ cup water
¾ cup cornmeal
2 tablespoons olive or peanut oil
1 bag fresh squash blossoms
salt to taste

Place the milk or the egg and water mixture in a small bowl. Place the cornmeal on a plate. Heat the oil over medium-high heat in a large skillet. Coat the squash blossoms first in the milk or egg mixture, then in cornmeal. Add the blossoms to the oil and cook until the cornmeal is golden, 3–5 minutes. Drain on paper towels and salt lightly. Use as an addition to tacos, or eat as snacks.

TOASTED PUMPKIN SEEDS (*PEPITAS*)

Raw pumpkin seeds are sold in *mercados* or in the bins of the bulk food section of large grocery stores. Toasted *pepitas* are wonderful for snacking, or as a taco topping.

2 teaspoons vegetable or peanut oil
1 cup shelled pumpkin seeds
salt (optional)

Heat oil in small skillet over medium-low heat. Add the pumpkin seeds and stir constantly until the seeds are browned and smell nutty, 5–6 minutes. Drain on paper towels and salt, if desired. Use immediately, or store in an airtight jar for up to a week.

Appendix: What Would You Find In Legacy's Galley?

WE ARE VERY LUCKY TO HAVE A WONDERFUL GALLEY ON LEGACY. She is a Saga 43 and Bob Perry's gracious design includes a spacious galley, which we are fond of saying is the only "two butt galley" we've ever seen on a 40–45 foot cruising sailboat. If you have less room in the galley, you'll need to make compromises about what you decide to carry on board. The list below of things that you would typically find aboard Legacy while cruising in Mexico will give you a starting point.

POTS AND PANS:

When we set up Legacy to go cruising, we realized that she was going to be our home for at least several years. Therefore, we decided that we weren't willing to make do with cheap, flimsy cookware. We brought some of our favorite items aboard from our house, and invested in a good set of Calphalon cookware for the boat. We've never regretted that decision. Below is a list of the pots and pans we have aboard:

Tea kettle
Nissan thermal French press coffeepot
Skillets, 10-inch—two, one nonstick and one regular
Omelet pan, 6-inch
Stovetop grilling pan
Lidded saucepans, 4 ranging in size from 1½ qt. to 8 qt.
Large crab or lobster cooking pot
Dutch oven or paella pan
Pressure cooker
Small broiler pan

8-inch square pans, 2
Loaf pans, 2
9 × 13 inch baking pan
Muffin pans, 2
Mini-muffin pans, 2
Pyrex custard cups, 4
9-inch pie plates, 2
Cookie sheets, 2 (make sure they fit in your oven!)
Colanders, 2
Nesting metal mixing bowls
Additional shallow metal bowls to use as serving bowls or use as a double boiler

UTENSILS

Liquid measuring cups, 2 cup and ¼ cup
Dry measuring cups, nested, ¼–1 cup
Measuring spoons, 2 sets
Coffee scoop
Knives—high quality set including chef's, paring, and serrated
Sharpening steel
Good kitchen scissors
Can openers, 2
Bottle opener
Wall-mount bottle opener (most Mexican beer is bottled)
Wine opener (corkscrew)
Vacu-vin wine bottle resealer and stoppers
Salt and pepper grinder
Instant read thermometer
Vegetable peeler
Pastry brush
French canning jar for Lemon Butter
Small glass jar for dressings
Tortilla warmers, 2
Bag clips
Skewers, metal and bamboo
Toothpicks
Wooden spoon
Whisks, 2
Silicone "spoonula"
Silicone spatula
Rice or wok spoon
Ladle
Slotted spoon
Pancake turners, 2

Micro-rasp style grater
Regular flat grater
Potato masher
Pie server
Tongs, 2—regular and long
Barbecue fork
Garlic press
Lime press
Mango splitter
English muffin rings
Wooden mallet
Butane "matches", 3
Funnels, 2 sizes
Ice pick
Rolling pin and pastry sheet
Assorted cutting boards
Large "airpot" style thermos
Melitta coffee filter cones and filters

APPLIANCES

We are lucky to have a built-in microwave on Legacy. If I didn't have one built in, I would be tempted to find a small microwave that I could fit in somewhere. It is very useful for heating up meals on passages, heating water to activate yeast, warming tortillas, defrosting meat, and melting butter. If you don't have a microwave, you may want to give some consideration to how you'll accomplish those normal chores that you don't think twice about on land. Other small electrical appliances we carry onboard are:

Small rice cooker
Small food processor
Hand mixer
Vacuum sealer

CHINA AND FLATWARE

As with our cookware, we decided that we didn't want to eat off of plastic plates every day. Although we have cheap plastic plates aboard to take to potlucks, our everyday china is a nice moderately-priced set of stoneware. When we purchased it, we bought two sets of 4 place settings. We keep 4 or 5 place settings handy and store the rest in a deeply buried locker. That way, when we inevitably break pieces we can easily replace them.

In addition to our stoneware, we carry several Corelle bowls in two sizes. These unbreakable bowls are great to hold ingredients, serve as small mixing bowls, or use for heating and serving meals underway.

Our flatware is nice, heavy stainless with a good feel to it. I refuse to live with cheap flatware that bends and breaks. We keep eight place settings on the boat along with serving pieces, four grapefruit spoons, and chopsticks.

Our "glasses" are clear, unbreakable Lexan. We carry six tall glasses and six wine glasses. We also have a few specialty glasses, such as small Mexican glasses for tequila, heavy duty plastic champagne flutes, insulated coffee mugs, and stainless steel martini glasses.

SERVING DISHES

Our first year aboard, I didn't have any good serving dishes. I quickly realized that potluck parties are a staple of the cruising life, so over the next couple of years I bought nice serving dishes as souvenirs of the places we visited. In most cities in Mexico you can buy painted ceramics that make nice serving pieces. Zihuatenejo is well known for beautiful, brightly painted wooden bowls and platters, which are even better because they are lightweight and unbreakable! I have three platters of various sizes and two bowls.

MISCELLANEOUS NONFOOD ITEMS

Folding dish drainer
Potholders, including neoprene mitt and potholder
Dish towels (lots)
Sponges (lots)
Tuffy scrubbers
Chlorine bleach
Dish soap
Paper towel holder
Nets and baskets to hold fruit
Kitchen timer
Large set of plastic storage containers ranging from ½ cup to 2 qt. size
Beverage containers, 3 pint, 1 quart, 1 half-gallon size
Tupperware sealable ice cube tray
Plastic egg containers, 2
Plastic butter container with sealable lid
Nalgene jars to hold dry goods
Plastic bottles to hold olive and canola oils
Oil misting bottle
Ziploc bags—snack size, sandwich size, quart, gallon, two-gallon, and veggie
Plastic wrap and aluminum foil
Extra FoodSaver bag material
Paper bags—lunch sack size
Small paper or plastic plates for serving appetizers or desserts to guests
Paper towels
Toilet paper
Kleenex
Paper napkins

Cloth placemats and napkins
Trash bags

STAPLES

I store all of my dry goods in wide-mouth Nalgene jars, in sizes ranging from 1 pint to 1 gallon. Nalgene seems to work well to keep food dry and bug-free. For extra protection, I put a few bay leaves into the containers that hold flour, cornmeal, Bisquick, and other grains.

Flour, all-purpose, 10 lb.
Sugar, 10 lb.
Cornmeal, 5 lb.
Bisquick, 2–3 large boxes
Cereal
Rolled oats, 1 box
Irish oatmeal, 1 can
Rice, 5 lb.
Baking soda
Baking powder
Cornstarch
Bread crumbs
Salt
Vanilla
Yeast (4-oz. jar)
Chicken and beef bouillon cubes
Tea
Hot chocolate mix
Coffee
Crystal Light beverage mixes
Peanut butter (lots)
Jams and marmalades, 3–4 jars
Shortening
Honey
Light corn syrup
Pancake syrup
Cocoa
Baking chocolate
Dates, raisins, dried cranberries, etc.
Assorted nuts for cooking: slivered almonds, walnuts, pecans

SPICES

I like having a variety of spices aboard, so probably devote more space to spice storage than most folks would tolerate. Most of the spices and all of the spice mixes listed below come from Penzey's Spices (www.penzeys.com). Except for a couple of heavily used items, I buy a ¼-cup plastic container of each spice.

Commonly Used Spices:

Allspice
Basil
Bay Leaf
Cayenne
Chili powder
Cinnamon
Cloves
Cumin
Curry Powder
Ginger
Italian Seasoning
Nutmeg
Oregano
Paprika
Smoked Paprika
Red Pepper Flakes
Rosemary
Tarragon
Thyme
Tumeric

Less Frequently Used Spices:

Caraway
Chipotle ground red pepper
Chives
Cilantro
Coriander, ground
Cream of Tartar
Dill
Epazote
Mint
Mustard Powder
Poppy Seeds
Saffron
Sesame Seeds

Specialty Spices and Spice Mixes:

Brady Street Cheese Sprinkle
Cake Spice

Chip and Dip Seasoning
Fajita Seasoning
Greek Seasoning
Horseradish Dip
Horseradish Powder

OILS, VINEGARS, AND CONDIMENTS

Canola oil (1 large bottle)
Olive oil (1 Costco twin-pack)
High quality extra-virgin olive oil for dressings
Sesame oil
Hot chili oil
Distilled white vinegar (1 large bottle)
Cider vinegar
White wine vinegar
Red wine vinegar
Balsamic vinegar
Worcestershire sauce
Soy sauce
Tabasco sauce
Salsa mexicana
Salsa picante
Salsa chipotle
Mole paste
Thai red curry paste
Ketchup
Dijon mustard
Pickle relish (2 jars)
Mayonnaise (3–4 small jars)
Caramel sauce

CANNED GOODS

Chicken broth, 12 cans
Diced tomatoes, 12–16 cans
Tomato sauce, 6 assorted size cans
Tomato paste, 6 small cans
Pasta sauce, 2–3 jars
Pizza sauce, 2–3 cans or jars
Kidney beans, 6–8 cans
Black beans, 2–3 cans
Black olives, 6 cans sliced, 6 cans chopped, 1 can whole
Stuffed green olives, 2 jars

Diced green chiles, 8–10 cans
Assorted soups, 4–6 cans
Canned corn
Canned green beans
Three bean salad
Crushed pineapple, 3–4 small cans
Mandarin oranges, 3–4 small cans
Tuna, several cans or pouches
Chicken or turkey, 2–3 cans
Roast beef hash
Smoked salmon, several small retort pouches or cans
Anchovies
Chilorio
Refried beans
Assorted pates and meat spreads
Prepared salsas, several small cans
Coconut milk, 2–3 cans
Pumpkin, 2–3 small cans
Evaporated milk, 3 large, 3 small cans
Nestle *Media Crema*, 3–4 cans
Sweetened condensed milk (*La Lechera*)
Aseptic packages milk, liter and individual size
Juice boxes, 12 assorted, individual size
Precooked shelf-stable bacon, 4 Costco packages

DRY GOODS

Assorted pasta (spaghetti, macaroni, rigatoni, fusilli, etc), several packages
Packaged side dishes (rice-a-roni, couscous, pasta, etc.), several packages
Mashed potato flakes, 2 boxes
Cookie mixes
Cornbread mixes
Brownie mixes
Muffin mixes
Macaroni and cheese mixes
Soup mixes
Pasta salad mixes

SNACK FOOD

Pistachios
Cashews
Dried apricots, dates, raisins, and other dried fruits
Tiger's Milk bars or granola bars
Pringles or potato chips

Tortilla chips
Microwave popcorn
Cookies
Crackers
Chocolate

DAIRY PRODUCTS, CHEESES, AND OTHER REFRIGERATED ITEMS

Butter
Sour cream or *crema*
Heavy cream (*crema para batir*) for cooking and to mix for half and half
Milk, both fresh (if available) and aseptic packages
Cream cheese
Hard grating cheese, such as Romano or Parmesan
Melting cheeses such as *asadero* and *Chihuahua*
Other cheese for nibbling, sandwiches, or cooking
Ham or turkey breast slices for sandwiches

FROZEN FOODS

Steaks
Ground beef
Arrachera
Lamb chops
Boneless lamb
Pork chops
Pork loin
Boneless chicken breasts
Boneless chicken thighs
Roast chicken
Chorizo
Pepperoni
Shrimp
Dorado filets
Peas
Extra butter

PRODUCE

We'll pick up other items for specific recipes, but we nearly always have on board the following fruits and vegetables:

Onions, white and red
Garlic

Limes
Tomatoes
Potatoes
Zucchini
Carrots
Bell peppers, red and green
Jalapeños
Avocados
Grapefruit
Fresh ginger (kept in freezer)

BEVERAGES, ALCOHOL, AND MIXERS

We keep a variety of beverages on hand, generally in smaller bottles, for entertaining, for cooking, and for personal consumption.

Assorted sodas
Pineapple juice
Orange juice
Tonic water
Wine, red and white
Beer
Rum
Tequila
Scotch
Gin
Vermouth
Port
Triple Sec or *Controy*
Kahlua
Brandy
Jarabe natural (sugar syrup)
Grenadine syrup

Index: